T0322379

KIN,
PEOPLE
OR
NATION?

This book is dedicated to Simona Neumann,
for her belief in the European idea and in recognition of her
leadership in winning the European Capital of Culture
title for Timișoara in 2023.

Victor NEUMANN

KIN, PEOPLE OR NATION?

On European Political Identities

With a Foreword by
Hans Erich BÖDEKER

Translated by
Gabi REIGH

Edited by
Neil TITMAN

SCALA

CONTENTS

ILLUSTRATIONS

Plates are located between pages 80 and 81.

Page 1

Jules Michelet. Oil painting by Thomas Couture, *c*.1865. (*Musée Carnavalet, Histoire de Paris / Paris Musées, http://parismuseescollections. paris.fr*)

Voltaire and Rousseau beneath the eye of the Supreme Being. Anonymous engraving, originally published by Paul André Basset (Fils), Paris, 1794. (*Musée Carnavalet, Histoire de Paris / Paris Musées, http://parismuseescollections. paris.fr*)

Page 2

Johann Gottfried Herder. Oil painting by Anton Graff, 1785. (*Gleimhaus. Museum der deutschen Aufklärung*)

Die Hermannsschlacht. Anonymous colour print after an oil painting by Friedrich Gunkel, 1862–4, in the Maximilianeum, Munich (destroyed 1943). (*akg-images Ltd*)

Page 3

République universelle démocratique et sociale: Le Pacte. Lithograph by Frédéric Sorrieu and Marie-Cécile Goldsmid, originally printed by Imprimerie Lemercier, Paris, 6 December 1848. (*Musée Carnavalet, Histoire de Paris / Paris Musées, http:// parismuseescollections.paris.fr*)

Wallachian revolutionaries with the Romanian tricolour, 1848. Engraving by Costache Petrescu, 1848. (*Biblioteca Academiei Române din București / Wikimedia Commons*)

Page 4

Ernest Renan. Photograph by Antoine Samuel Adam-Salomon, 1876–84. (*LACMA*)

Kaiserproklamation am 18 Januar 1871. Oil painting by Anton von Werner, completed 1 April 1885. (*Otto-von-Bismarck-Stiftung / Wikimedia Commons*)

Page 5

Mosque and marketplace, Sarajevo. Stereograph (detail) by Keystone View Company, c.1910. (*Library of Congress, Washington, DC*)

The Moda cricket team, Istanbul. Photographer unidentified, 1896. (*Levantine Heritage Foundation, Istanbul*)

Page 6

Romanian Catholic Bishop Iuliu Hossu reading the declaration of the union of Transylvania with Romania, Alba Iulia. Photographer unidentified, 1 December 1918. (*Wikimedia Commons*)

Inspection of the Iron Guard by its leader and founder, Corneliu Zelea Codreanu, Romania. Photographer unidentified, c.1934. (*Photo by Keystone / Hulton Archive / Getty Images*)

Page 7

US President Gerald R. Ford, Romanian President Nicolae Ceaușescu, First Lady Betty Ford and Mrs Elena Ceaușescu with 'folk dancers', Piața Victoriei, Bucharest. Photographer unidentified, 8 February 1975. (Gerald R. Ford White House Photographs, 8/9/1974–1/20/1977, White House Photographic Office Collection (*Ford Administration) / National Archives Catalog*)

Demonstrators against President Nicolae Ceaușescu, Bulevardul Revoluției din 1989 (formerly Bulevardul 23 August), Timișoara. Photograph by Constantin Duma for AGERPRES, 20 December 1989. (*Courtesy of Constantin Duma*)

Page 8

Hungarian Jobbik party representatives demonstrating at Poland's annual National Independence Day march in Warsaw. Photograph by Janek Skarżyński, 11 November 2015. (JANEK SKARZYNSKI / AFP *via Getty Images*)

Liberté guidant le peuple 2019. Mural by Pascal Boyart, 105 rue d'Aubervilliers, Paris (18ᵉ arrondissement), *in situ* January–February 2019. (© *Pascal Boyart, 'Liberté guidant le peuple 2019', Paris*)

FOREWORD

Against the backdrop of the worrying return and spread of nationalism in the form of strong cultural and political identity, Victor Neumann approaches from a new perspective the unity–diversity relationship within and between cultural and political communities. His study combines historical and systematic moments of analysis of national thinking and arguing in order to problematise the concept of nation.

His historiographical chapters construe the semantic field 'nation' – its constitutive moments, effects and supporters – explaining the nation state in France, the cultural nation in the historical German-speaking regions of the nineteenth century, and in Eastern Europe with a particular focus on twentieth-century Romania. His approach subtly considers the use of the semantic field by distinct speakers in distinct circumstances for distinct purposes.

The systematically oriented chapters build on the critical reconsideration of some remarkable theorists of those categories that had shaped the discussion about the 'nation' for a long time, such as identity, unity, diversity, ethnicity, culture, etc. They, however, turned out to be inadequate for both a plausible analysis of the historical processes under consideration and a conceptualisation of the contemporary world, since they presuppose uniform, homogeneous and closed cultural and political communities. Neumann regards the need to redefine these patterns of analysis as inevitable. His close look at these categories demonstrates that identity is always hybrid, that culture is always heterogeneous and that historical differences are not just exclusive. Cultures unfold, he convincingly argues, in the tension between diversity and what they have in common. According to Neumann, the political and cultural world is characterised by being individual and diverse at the same time.

Neumann's book is a substantial plea for the recognition of the other, of the other's culture, of the other's political community. Reciprocity, however, constitutes an essential prerequisite for recognition as a fundamental model for socio-political life.

Hans Erich Bödeker

PREFACE

Our understanding of the history, culture and politics of Europe, the Americas, Asia, Africa and Australia is enhanced by an investigation into the affiliations that transcend religious, linguistic and national bonds. In modern Europe, countries such as Great Britain, the Netherlands, France, Austria and, more recently, Germany, Italy and Spain possess a complex identity connected to a continuous process of immigration. If we consider Europe as a whole, we notice that it is characterised by linguistic and ideological interchange, parallels between religious traditions and a shared notion of civilisation and codes of behaviour passed down through history as evidence of a common cultural heritage.[1] All these reflect the fluid identity of individuals, groups and nations. The discovery of these shared characteristics enables us to reject the doctrine of our Romantic predecessors and their emphasis on what divides, versus what unites us. We understand that both individual and collective identity are heterogeneous rather than specific, viewing them through the prism of plurality instead of singularity. The relationship between the local and the universal prompts us to be wary of coercive ideologies promoted by majority or minority groups.

Marc Bloch has described history as the sum of countless fruitful encounters between people and the narrative of their multiple experiences. He adds that life and science have been enriched by these brotherly connections. In any case, the rewriting of history cannot draw only on a single interpretation, a so-called 'accurate story', because there are multiple versions of the past.[2] History is not a linear narrative, but a collection of interconnected stories. In his study on the heterogeneity of Central European cultures, Moritz Csáky suggests it is important to take into consideration contradictory dates, facts and ideas and those that occurred through chance. His definition of collective identity takes into account the complexity of social, political and cultural life, implying that to conceptualise the past and the present, we must include diverse elements that go beyond the political and national as they may contradict communitarian and 'distinctly national' ideas.

The study of the evolution and fluid connotations of concepts such as freedom, culture, identity, community, people, nation, homeland, history, ideology and politics alerts us to the way language and ideas have been perpetually renewed as a result of social and political dynamics over the past two centuries.

By studying the ever-changing connotations of these terms, we become aware of the way that a new society appropriates such concepts and, by reinventing them, replaces the old order and undermines its credibility. By interrogating and evaluating its history, a society reconstructs itself. The theoretical legacy of the past is investigated by decoding such concepts and their equivalents so they can be reconsidered from the perspective of contemporary social science. For example, the concepts of kin, people and nation have taken on different connotations during various historical periods and reflected moments of emancipation, glory and tragedy. The majority of these connotations were not developed solely in the political realm, but were shaped by cultural and social phenomena in a specific context. As the discourse of identity is reinvented from one decade to another – for example, there has been a transition from the concept of the nation to the idea of a unified Europe – it will require fresh historical, political, philosophical and anthropological interpretations.

There are many linguistic cultures that analyse the diverse meanings of concepts, language and messages. For example, a positive evolution took place in Spanish culture when the notion of patriotism became tied to constitutional aspects ('*el patriotismo de la constitución*') instead of defining the identity of an ethnonational group. Javier Fernández Sebastián and Juan Francisco Fuentes have discussed the controversial aspects of this concept and its impact on the relationship between various social groups, at the same time as drawing attention to problems arising from the ambiguous application of certain terms.[3] Adapting Spain's notion of identity to the changing times can be seen as a step in the right direction. By considering the way that the concepts of kin, people and nation have been used in Central and Southeastern European culture and comparing them to Franco-German notions of *peuple*, *nation*, *Volk*, *Völkischekultur* and *Kulturnation*, we can trace their influence on the intelligentsia and the masses. Interwar ethnonationalism and nationalism as well as national-Communist protochronism (as experienced by Romania, Serbia and Bulgaria) had their roots in nineteenth-century Romanticism and motivate the contemporary intelligentsia's reinvention of political identity in accordance with the European federal project.

There are no ideal definitions, only contradictions created by semantic change. Nevertheless, we should attempt to discover the experience beyond language and clarify the notions and categories that indicate the real or illusory cultural identity of the individual, citizen or society. An illusory sense of identity can be stimulated by false messages which, although devoid of reality, appeal to human emotions and instincts and thus imprint themselves onto the collective consciousness. In such cases, the presentation of the past and present political context is phantasmagorical,[4] and is employed to the benefit of the dominant minority, privileging one particular section of society at the same time as disadvantaging all others. The semantics of history reveal the two key resources of modern politics: language and time. Instead of adopting the most transparent approach, politicians and intellectuals are often wary when discussing the question of language, illustrating the importance of constructing historiographical and sociological disciplines that are more reflexive, less dogmatic, less ideologically laden and less linear.

When discussing the diverse world of earlier generations it is necessary to bear in mind the limits of the social sciences and submit them to critical and rational analysis. The questions raised in this book attempt to problematise the concept of the nation and reconsider the impact of our diverse cultural heritage and political theories. I have considered the different connotations of the concept of nation, taking into account origins, language, religion, territoriality, administration, legislation and civic identity. Questions regarding individual and group identity are particularly pertinent considering the close correlation between dominant political ideologies and the idea of the nation. The civic nation is not the same as the cultural nation, hence administrative and legal matters are separate from ideas about language and collectivity. The concept of the nation has been omnipresent in social and political discourse over the past two centuries, but we should not ignore the multicultural and intercultural realities of those societies and should acknowledge that their 'fusion of horizons' can help us redefine the notion of identity. This is why I argue that European nation states would be advised to renounce some of their sovereignty for the benefit of a transnational federation.

Kin, People or Nation? is a survey of some of the most influential works on history and political philosophy and aims to reveal the significant impact of Romantic and post-Romantic thought on the segregation of Europe and its people on the basis of ethnocultural and national criteria. On the other hand, further research indicates the survival of an opposite idea, that of integration, which illustrates the possibility of transcending cultural and linguistic divides through administrational and legal efforts. The success of this enterprise relies on our familiarisation with past and present multicultural and intercultural realities, as well as the old utopian ideals we have inherited from the most illustrious Renaissance and Enlightenment thinkers whose imagination contrived the first image of modern Europe.[5] The importance and even urgency of grasping these realities will be apparent to readers of this new English translation of the book, which is being published at a time when the notion of European integration finds itself under great pressure from the forces of populism in many countries. While the later chapters of this study focus on Eastern Europe and my native Romania in particular, the ideas and the challenges I discuss will resonate strongly with audiences across Europe and beyond.

Victor Neumann, 2021

I

JULES MICHELET'S CONCEPT OF PEUPLE

1. COMMENTARY ON ITS ORIGINS AND MEANINGS

I will begin by defining the concept of *peuple*, as it is central to various new theories of identity, in the sense that it reveals the foundations of France's quest for social harmony. My aim is to analyse this ideology and its impact on contemporary and modern political thought. Arguably, this concept has often been misunderstood and inappropriately applied to other societies whose cultures and political systems are different from those of France. For example, the Romanian *popor*, the Slavic *narod* and the Hungarian *nép* are all words that have been mistakenly equated with *peuple*. The aforementioned cultures adopted the French term as a way of consolidating their own myths of national identity, but in doing so they diluted its original meaning. The most important goal for those nations was the formulation of autonomous political and linguistic communities distinct from others around them. As a result of this loose application of the concept of *peuple* to a wide variety of contexts, a range of theories have emerged about the nature of Eastern and Western national identities. By exploring the true meaning of the language used to define them, it is possible to gain a deeper understanding of contemporary political debates relating to nationhood.

My argument will not focus on the violent conflicts between nations or ethnic groups during the totalitarian regimes of the twentieth century. The purpose of this section is merely to explore the intellectual foundations of a specific myth of national identity. By tracing this myth back to its origins, we begin to understand the role it has played in shaping modern European political thought. This concept was not borrowed by the French from any other languages or cultures. Any external influences, if they even existed, were seamlessly assimilated into France's specific context, namely conditions there during the eighteenth and nineteenth centuries. The concept of *peuple* was born out of social and economic realities, and is inseparable from the institutions established during the French Revolution. Historiographers have commented on connections between the revolutionary ideal of *peuple* and the ideology of nationhood forged in the medieval era. These parallels are used to amplify the general ideology of national belonging that has run through the course of France's history.

It would be unwise to create too rigid a distinction between the ideology of *peuple* and that of *nation*. However, as the development of political discourse is shaped by these shifts in language, it is worth making some observations regarding the differences between these concepts. The distinction between *peuple* and *nation* has its roots in the radical politics of 1789. In effect, our definition of these terms is connected to the social landscape of France at the end of the eighteenth century and the seismic changes brought about by the Revolution. At the time a new political identity was conceived. A historico-political analysis of the word *peuple* suggests that it refers to the masses, to the emotional state of a population, to a national spirit that exists as a continuum between the past and present. *Nation,* on the other hand, has more clearly defined parameters: it refers to the social, judicial and historical aspects of the state.[1]

Whereas *le peuple* – like *das Volk* – implies the idea of a community, *nation* entails a more complex system, such as a society organised by a state, an entity with a coherent political purpose, exercised both internally and externally. *Nation* transcends the local sphere, it goes beyond regional concerns or traditions, its aims are universal. This distinction applies to a number of other languages and cultures: French, British and Dutch, for example. The concept of *le peuple* – similarly to *das Volk* – makes sense only in a particular linguistic community.[2] It is a construct inextricably tied to a specific moment in French history, and to ignore this is to lose some of its nuances and connotations, which are linked to certain cultural and religious traditions. With some exceptions, most historians do not distinguish between the concepts of *peuple* and *nation* in the case of France or between *das Volk* and *die Nation* in relation to Germany. Despite the fact that these terms have often been regarded as interchangeable, we should consider in more detail their different connotations. For instance, it can be said that by equating the French *la nation* with the German *die Nation*, we overlook the political traditions that have given rise to these terms and the ideological conflicts between them. Likewise, by conflating the French *peuple* with the German *Volk* or the Slavic *narod* or the Romanian *popor*, the political cultures of these countries begin to lose their distinctness. If we accept these preliminary observations, we can infer not only that these terms have been misused by Central and Eastern European countries in an attempt to define their social history, but that the West has been equally guilty of applying these paradigms to every culture, regardless of its unique traditions or political situation.

In his preface to the third volume of *Les Lieux de mémoire*, Pierre Nora perceptively observes that a sense of identity feeds on its own contradictions, that it must acknowledge political, religious and geo-historical conflicts. He notes certain schisms within modern, contemporary identities, which he attributes to contrasting religious, political, social and national ideas that emerged in 1789. The notion of *peuple* became pivotal as it was associated with the possibility of political renewal after the fall of the monarchy. *Peuple* became emblematic of the sovereignty of the state. This concept, which assumed an enormous transformation of the body politic and the public sphere, came at a crucial moment in French history and its echoes are still felt today. It would compete with the cultural and religious narratives that shaped that country. In 1789 France was not interested in the resurgence of any particular ethnic group or in creating a sense of unity between members of one particular race. At that moment in history, the main priority was the elevation of the status of the masses and the imperative that they should play a significant role in its history. From this context the concept of *peuple* emerged.

The historian Jacques Julliard argues that social division was the catalyst of political upheaval in France. However, this disruption did not resolve the problem. In France, 'Class struggles never turned into a general confrontation due to the pre-existence of the republican political structure'. This paradox strikes him as irritating, as he sees France simultaneously as 'the *enfant terrible* of the nineteenth-century revolutionaries and the embodiment of systematic deception'.[3]

The French Revolution generated several versions of *le peuple*: 1. *peuple-nation*, which refers to the whole population, regardless of social class – this is Mirabeau's *le peuple*; 2. *le peuple-tiers état*, which entails abolition of the aristocracy and transfer of power to the intellectual bourgeoisie, a version favoured by Sieyès; 3. *le peuple des travailleurs*, which is a more informal descriptor of a society centred around the working class, such as labourers, shopkeepers or anyone who belongs to the mass of the Parisian poor; 4. *le peuple des bras nus et des miséreux*, an even less inclusive term that was briefly used in 1789. 'It does not announce a new era of history, but bears witness to the political and economic changes of that period and highlights the plight of the socially excluded.'[4]

2. MICHELET'S INTERROGATIONS

In this section, we consider Jules Michelet's role in defining the concept of *peuple* through his works. By delineating *le peuple* and *la nation*, his writings had considerable impact on historiography and French political culture: in short, his *Histoire de France* (*History of France*, 1833) outlined the origins and evolution of French society. His studies at the École Normale inspired him to re-evaluate the past. The essay *Le Peuple* (*The People*) focuses on defining this particular concept. In addition, his final book returns to this topic and consolidates its legendary status for posterity. For these reasons, Michelet was hailed as a hero by ardent revolutionaries. The entire course of history was changed by questions he raised on the subject of identity:

1) How did Europe become so widely populated?
2) How can populations trace their origins if it is impossible to tell the distinctions between groups before the Middle Ages?
3) Have certain groups always shared a united identity and language at any given moment in history?
4) How do we explain the coalition of various ethnicities or races, and how has this fusion contributed to the birth of the concept of *peuple*?
5) What are the factors that further social cohesion?
6) What value should we place on the ideology of *peuple*?
7) To what extent is history a narrative of spiritual evolution?[5]

Michelet moved away from the vision of the past contrived in the Enlightenment and offered a fresh perspective. Whereas his predecessors had evaluated history through the lens of rationality, he restored the importance of myth. 'France is founded on principles and legend,' he wrote. By 'principles' he means 'brotherhood', and by 'legend' he alludes to a glorious tradition harking back to Caesar, Charlemagne, Louis XIV and Napoleon, all of them integral to France's identity. His argument merges the rational with the sentimental, revealing all the different factors that created the bond between individuals and society. Through this, he unearthed the roots of specific traditions, investigating the influence of Christianity and Roman civilisation on the French state. These roots were to play an essential role in formulating the myth of France. By calling upon religious traditions, Michelet proposed an ideal based on community spirit rather than bourgeois individualism. His motto was to become 'France is a religion'. His Romantic spirit denounced the histories of Italy, Germany and Britain as 'mutilated', while proclaiming that France would serve as an example to all, describing it as the only 'great tradition' with progressive values.

The concept of *peuple* was to embody all the qualities necessary to the construction of a new social and political order. Despite his Romantic approach to history, Michelet understood that it was imperative that the fractures in France's social and political networks caused by the 1789 revolution needed to heal. This was the chief impetus that led to the transformation of *peuple* into an overarching myth of brotherhood and solidarity.[6]

3. CHALLENGING THIERRY'S ARGUMENTS

While formulating his ideology, Michelet attempted to find a balance between contemporary ideals and the historico-political realities of the nineteenth century. His writings were influenced by his own experiences as well as his intellectual and spiritual aspirations. They were the product of arduous study and rigorous debate with his mentors. For a significant period of time Michelet was a disciple of Augustin Thierry: he read much of his work and assimilated his philosophical theories on history. While Thierry wrote that there was a sense of cohesion between France's national identity and its government, he observed this had not always been the case.

Thierry challenged historical approaches that failed to take into account the distinctions between different nations and therefore ignored their diverse origins:

> History should expose the differences between cultures as well as their similarities... Unfortunately, mediocre thinkers are prone to generalisation: generalisations make them feel comfortable! But they are also deceptive, they create a false image of the past which makes it difficult to scrutinise. Our wise, revered historians dream of a unified history; they use the same language to describe a variety of contexts; for them, *peuple* means the same thing every time, it is their Ariadne's thread, the key to the identity of any society. But the real Ariadne's thread, were they to seek for it, would lead them on a different path. They would discover the origins of nations by studying their languages, their ways of living and thinking.[7]

Thierry identified only some of the elements that contributed to the definition of *peuple*, surprisingly overlooking the impact of the 1789 revolution. His first attempt at articulating the spirit of French identity strikes me as maladroit due to its overemphasis on the relationship between language and origins. Thierry was a product of his time, hence his theory is tinged with political ideology. This historico-political approach initially seduced Michelet, at least during his time as a teacher at the École Normale. Thierry's writings acted as his first introduction to political science. Michelet was attracted to the idea that history could help us interpret the present, the future might be mirrored in the past, and our beginnings might point to our final destination.

At first, Michelet truly believed that Thierry had formulated an entirely new and coherent interpretation of events and that he was not interested in writing the history of any particular ethno-linguistic group. One of Michelet's theories adopted from Thierry was that races survive amalgamation and preserve their distinct character. As a result, the influences of these racial traits will always be felt in any given community throughout its history.[8] This emphasis on racial origins intrigued the young scholar captivated by a desire to understand French identity. Similar reflections abound in Thierry's work, for example the idea that nature, matter and destiny can be traced back to racial heredity. As a result, it was some time before Michelet adopted the German Romantic view regarding parallels between the microcosm and the macrocosm.

In the first volume of his *Histoire de France*, Michelet echoes Thierry's arguments, even conflating *race* with *peuple*, based on the idea that race speaks of a continuous identity over a long period of time. But these convictions were shaken by the time he wrote the next volumes of the *Histoire de France*. As soon as he realised that human communities are constantly in flux, that they do not exist in isolation and therefore will necessarily diverge from their origins, Michelet began to theorise about national identity in a way that set him apart from Thierry. He argued that the development of a community is similar to the emancipation of a child under parental guidance and eventually concluded that the masses shape their own nebulous racial identity.

Michelet offered an important revelation, realising that both the primitive genius of the Celts and foreign influences played equally significant roles in the development of France's origins. The concept of *peuple* could not therefore be based on ethnic or racial purity. The Celts, for example, not only contributed to the formation of the French nation, but also held sway in Rome, Greece and Germany:

Who unified all these disparate elements, who moulded them into a body, thus transfiguring them? Only France, which absorbed them into its inner structures, which merged them together into a mysterious combination of necessity and liberty. The primitive seed germinates over time, during the course of history. The French nation triumphs over racial differences to be hailed the heroic champion of liberty.[9]

We must assume that such reflections would not have been conceived by Thierry. There is a different political ideology at work in Michelet's definition of *peuple*. The 'mysterious combination of necessity and liberty' implies a unified consciousness, and for him it is not the 'primitive seed' that shapes the political entity, but rather 'the course of history'. Michelet's conclusion is unequivocal: for a nation to claim the title of 'the heroic champion of liberty', it must move beyond its racial origins and see itself as the product of a historical evolution.

Michelet does not come close to the level of Renan's analysis in *Qu'est-ce qu'une Nation?* (*What is a Nation?*) which we will discuss below. He does not go so far as to reject the illusory connection between politics and ethnography.[10] Nevertheless, his refusal to explain French history by delving into its ethnographic origins became a defining feature of his work. His re-evaluation implies that Thierry is guilty of a moral lapse when he equates identity with race. Such an approach, Michelet claims, betrays the very essence of humankind, which after all is the subject of history. It is said that Michelet began his career believing that race was connected to national identity, then later rejected the notion. In fact, writing about Britain's history as early as 1829, he criticised Thierry's tendency to analyse socio-cultural and political entities through the prism of race. Even at the beginning of his didactic and historiographic enterprise, Michelet asserted that 'if we assume that our whole history has developed from our primitive origins [meaning race], we relinquish our freedom'.[11]

What differentiates Michelet from Thierry – the mentor of his youthful self – is the concept of free will as the element that governs human life. Not only does he reject the idea that *race* is at the heart of social structures, Michelet also endows the concept of *peuple* with the ability to dissolve racial differences. In the *Histoire de France*, he only draws attention to these diverse elements in order to highlight how they can be sacrificed and assimilated into a community.[12] According to Michelet, conflicts for racial supremacy reached their peak in late antiquity and the Middle Ages. In the following era, *peuple* held sway. In the *Histoire de France* he describes how the beginning of his country's history was characterised by the invasion of different tribes (or races) who settled, one after another, on this Gallic land. After the Celts came the Romans and, finally, the Germans. These are the elements from which the national community was born. The next stage was the assimilation of these races into something that might be called society.

4. WHEN *LE PEUPLE* BECOMES *LA NATION*

Guided by his own ideological leanings, Michelet did not grant the title of *peuple* to either the Romans or the Greeks. He berated those ancient socio-political entities for their practice of slavery, their lack of interest in the development of the citizen and their tendency towards brutal domination as opposed to the encouragement of kinship or spiritual bonds. These reassessments of the past were coloured by personal judgements that conformed to contemporary values, and are not particularly illuminating with regard to the workings of those ancient societies.

The concept of *peuple* was imbued with many meanings. Arguably, these were shaped by a number of historical approaches reflecting the development of political thought. For example, Michelet believed there was a hierarchy of human communities that had varying capacities for social assimilation. In modern times, their history has oscillated between the same setbacks and successes. This is exemplified through a comparison of England and France. While in England there would have been an incomplete fusion of races, in France this was perceived as their crowning achievement. Hence the conclusion: '*Le peuple des peuples est le peuple français*' (The people of peoples is the French people).

Michelet drew comparisons between modern and ancient societies. He did not establish direct connections between them, as we see in the case of German historiography. He used the example of Switzerland and its emphasis on the role of the homeland in structuring the Swiss nation to illustrate the importance of the common organisation and administration of a territory.

While for Herder and his German-speaking peers the concept of *Volk* reflected uniqueness and racial unity, *peuple* consolidated various social, cultural, religious and racial components that had coexisted for centuries. Renan would go further in defining identity and acknowledged Michelet's special contribution, particularly the multiple connotations that the revolutionary historian attributed to the concept of *peuple*.[13] Michelet's most significant achievement was his attempt to create a theoretical framework through which to interpret contemporary France.

Michelet's definition of *peuple* was shaped by his interpretation of the French Revolution as well as his personal experiences. For these reasons, he endowed the concept with a symbolic power. Michelet's *peuple* is similar to the concept of *la nation* and could even be considered its foundation. *Peuple* becomes *nation* once it navigates the hazards of heredity and geography and manages to combine them successfully. *Nation*, therefore, is the product of the toil of the *peuple*. The first step of *peuple* developing into *nation* is when everyone becomes equal in the eyes of the law. The second stage is when each citizen feels protected and has opportunities to develop. According to Michelet, *nation* could not have existed in the Middle Ages due to a lack of means of communication. As exemplified by France, we see that *peuple* can exist only in a well-established community and comes at a fairly late stage in its social and political development. Michelet's message seems to be: 'A *nation* is a *peuple* that understands itself.' Prompted by this observation, French historian Paul Viallaneix draws parallels between France and other European states at various points in history. While it is reasonable to assume that there may be similarities between the respective developments of these countries, it would be dangerous to overstate them given their many differences in the nineteenth century.

Many European countries developed into nations later than France due to their particular political and social circumstances. Europe was not France and France was not Europe, not in 1789, nor in 1848, nor later. In his enthusiasm, Michelet assumed that humanity was moulded in the image of France and that all the world shared its aspirations. Unfortunately, he was mistaken. Towards its centre and periphery, Europe was a land of different ideals and more modest economic conditions, where large sectors of the population were illiterate. In such countries, cultural and religious traditions played a different role in their transition towards modernity. The influences of Tsarist Russia, the Hapsburg Monarchy and the Ottoman Empire, as well as the absence of the kind of governmental structures that gave rise to the French *peuple*, are examples of the specific conditions that affected these communities. Furthermore, modernisation occurred at different speeds from region to region and although, like France, some of these countries also experienced revolutions, the stakes were not the same. Consequently, the changes that took place in these regions of Europe in 1848 might have led to political, but not social, transformations.

Michelet believed that as soon as peoples understood their own natures, they would overthrow their tyrants. In his view, this was the reason they asserted their national identities in the midst of bloody revolutions, as this was the revelatory moment when the masses became aware of their power. In this context, Michelet saw nationalism as justified: 'The modern world is characterised by the solidarity of the masses coming together, unified by the concept of *peuple*, insisting on their national identity until such a time as they become completely united into a single body, like a soul facing its Maker.'[14]

Michelet saw the mass uprising against monarchical tyranny in the French Revolution as a specifically modern event. Later, this unification of the masses would lead to the construction of democracy. These observations led him to consider *le peuple* as an expression of the democratic spirit. He would be one of the first to attribute two connotations to this concept: a historical one, which allowed the inclusion or exclusion of different sections of the population, and a pluralist one, which implied that *peuple* can transcend social distinctions. The first definition gave rise to nationalism, the second to democracy. French Romantic nationalism, especially the kind that derived from Michelet's ideology of *peuple*, had little in common with its German counterpart. Although its discourse invoked the land, the nation and the state, it did not insist on the importance of blood ties. Michelet equated *le peuple* with faith in the nation, thus constructing the myth of France's 1789 reunification. Unlike *das Volk*, he does not place *le peuple* on the throne of *jus sanguinis*, as was the case with German Romanticism. Instead, he discusses the nature of collective identity and the psychology of the masses as well as the value of medieval lore, but he does not emphasise the ethnic, racial and linguistic differences between groups. His nationalism is a social ideal, whereby the course of history proves the significance of territorial unity. He sees nothing in the past – not in its old political structures, important historical figures, heroes or religious practices – that poses a challenge to the harmony created through the coupling of *peuple* with *nation*.

Michelet wished to disassociate himself from other interpretations of collective identity. He criticised the German and Anglo-Saxon cultures for failing to achieve social harmony. What made these countries different from France? The discord between life and principles, as well as a tendency to present themselves as role models to the rest of the world and persuade them to adopt their teachings.[15] Expansionism of Prussia and Britain in the nineteenth century is seen to reflect these same cultural and political aims. On the other hand, he believes that France is mainly concerned with universal human problems, that she embraces anyone who gravitates towards her. In the foundation of the new state, Michelet's *peuple* was to become social pedagogy, giving rise to a modern nation:

> The day *le peuple* will become fully conscious of itself and open its eyes wide, it will comprehend that the first institution with any verve or longevity will be one that can offer everyone a harmonious education, as this is the foundation of any country and every child's heart. If God chooses to save this glorious, wretched country, it will be through its innocence.[16]

The blueprints of this new world were created after the French Revolution of 1789, through the Constituent Assembly and the Legislative Assembly. Michelet approved of the way universal education was decreed by these institutions born out of the Revolution. This education, which was intended to be available to different layers of society, was seen as a tool of emancipation and key to the formation of a modern nation. Michelet steered away from metaphysical discourse when describing changes brought about by the Revolution.[17] Why is the nation based on the concept of *peuple* different from that founded by *Volk*? Michelet quotes a passage from the report from the Convention: 'Time is the Republic's sole teacher'. He states that these words were intended to rein in impatient tempers. The revolutionaries were to understand that anyone of a high status would be obliged to take up the lowly position of the instructor. One by one, political leaders, civil servants and scholars devoted themselves to the establishment of schools and recognised that the French needed to be taught science before history or philosophy.[18] Michelet's argument revealed that the basic principle on which French identity was built differed from its German counterpart.

The inconsistencies in Michelet's argument are due to his imprecise use of language. Guizot criticised his poetic style. Despite such reservations, it can be said that the revolutionary historian had the incontestable merit of raising an important topical theme and inspiring an entire generation.

Michelet considered his greatest inspiration to be the philosopher Giambattista Vico, whose work *Scienza Nuova* (*New Science*) shaped his view of history and his political thinking. From Vico, Michelet inherited his view of humanity as a master of destiny, engaged in a constant quest to win its moral and social liberty. He took note of his predecessor's reflections on language, myths and the variety of social, economic and spiritual practices of the past. Some have even argued that Vico completely changed Michelet's way of thinking.[19] In reality, Michelet adopted only the notions that chimed with his own view of history. This accounts for the fact that the French translation of *Scienza Nuova* owes more to Michelet than to Vico.[20] Nevertheless, it should be noted that Michelet sees his own opinions mirrored in three key principles conceived by his Enlightenment forerunner: his belief in the existence of Providence, the importance of tempering our passions and nurturing our virtues, and, finally, the immortality of the soul.[21] Michelet's conception of the *peuple* myth, his elaboration of a Romantic-nationalist ideology and his insight into the issue of origins are all indebted to Vico.[22] This could explain the rhetorical bent of his historical analysis, which sought to inspire his revolutionary comrades.

The concept of *peuple* would gain unparalleled significance during the time of the 1848 revolution and for ensuing generations. It is a principle that transcends race and national belonging. At its heart are the assimilation of races, the desire to build a homeland

and the union between body and soul. The connotations of *peuple* diverge enormously from those of *Volk*, whose elements can be observed in terms such as *popor* (kin), *narod* or *nép*. For example, despite expressing their admiration for the principles proclaimed in Paris in 1848, the revolutionaries of Central, East-Central and Southeastern Europe did not apply the spirit of *le peuple* to their countries of origin. Naturally, it could be argued that it is merely a matter of translation, that these terms essentially mean the same thing. But Michelet was wrong to think that form does not affect content. In reality, the connotations of the concept change in each language and reflect different aspirations. For example, if we take the ideological roots of Romanian *popor-naţiune* or Hungarian *nép-nemzet*, we notice that they do not only describe social structures but, more importantly, organic entities. In such cases, the most essential priorities were (and in some cases, still are) a unified state and territorial independence. Their attention was largely focused on creating a distinct consciousness to set them apart from their neighbours, an awareness realised through language, religion and ethnographic traditions, while the emancipation and transformation of their communities was a lesser priority. In particular, the regions formerly part of the Austro-Hungarian Empire were set on this course in the latter decades of the nineteenth century. As a result, a segregationist and conservative spirit was in full force until the end of the Second World War.[23]

Eastern European countries did not always comprehend that the concept of *peuple* – and in particular the model of nationhood it dictated – derived from the ideology of equality conceived by Michelet. In the case of France, this concept paved the way for a society in which people from every social sphere were equal, autonomous and participating in public life. Where Michelet was a staunch believer in the emancipation of the masses and the socio-political role of *le peuple*, his counterparts in East-Central and Southeastern Europe used his concept to promote division between different ethnic groups.

5. THE SOCIAL MYTH

Michelet was not the only scholar to explore the social trends of his era. However, his ideas were a prelude to an inclusive, democratic new world. The spirit of democracy was enriched by his revolutionary historical works. These writings, like those of other political thinkers of his time, were fuelled by Romantic fervour but, according to Paul Viallaneix, they also played an important role in defining a myth at the heart of the political philosophy of the modern state.

Michelet's ideology was centred on the role of the individual and the power of the masses. He was not interested in history per se, but rather wanted to tell 'the story of a fight against the forces that wish to suppress liberty'.[24] Although he was a staunch supporter of the masses, Michelet did not idealise them and even recognised their flaws. He acknowledged their torpor, their sickness and their moral failings, but insisted that these were superficial vices, distracting us from their true nature. According to Michelet, the spirit of *le peuple* is tenacious, as we can see when it is channelled into military energy, valour and the struggle for independence. Its redeeming feature is that it is always on the side of right:

> One of the supposed virtues of the French is the ability to keep a cool head in moments of crisis and not be governed by emotions. However, *le peuple* celebrates instinctive passions, which are then channelled into decisive action. Such actions are often hindered by slow, rational deliberation which is nevertheless prone to errors of judgement. In contrast, spontaneity results in immediate action, it virtually embodies it; we might describe it as the fusion of an idea and a process.[25]

Acting instinctively provides a shortcut between abstraction and the deed. This is one of the reasons why Michelet felt so emotionally drawn to the masses. He was interested in their particular mode of reasoning, which he considered to be just as perceptive and valuable as the acumen of the old aristocracy. However, the marginalisation of the intellectual elite came at a price, as the inability to engage them in debate slowed down the emancipation of ordinary people. Michelet disapproved of the way the latter were punished for their alleged lack of civility: 'The powers that be do not want to represent you because they fear your incivility.' A bridge had to be built between the scholars and the impulsive masses:

> Those we might call the inferior classes are led by instinct, and this compels them to action... We scholars, on the other hand, are prone to endless analysis and debate, we battle with words and hotly disagree about the most trivial problems... Meanwhile, these [simple] people, being closer to nature, dare to strive and to dream. Young men's dreams seep into the wise, temperate reflections of their elders. Scholars like us pride ourselves on our ability to discuss and construct arguments, but in fact even for us it is life, with its pleasures and its trivial conversations, that holds the greatest attraction and makes us wish we could be freed from such intellectual constraints.[26]

What are we to conclude from this? Was the reasoning of Michelet's revolutionary comrades indeed flawed? Was it time for their intellectual and political perspectives to change? Michelet had a special relationship with the common people, with whom he felt a sense of solidarity and empathy for their struggles. Commoners were seen as important because they had always stood by their intellectual and political leaders. The Revolution was the time of their emancipation. Michelet understood that the old order was obsolete, that it was time for a transfer of power to the masses, as they would become the new champions of the state. He noted that the rebirth of the nation could not take place without the efforts of the largest sector of the population which included peasants, labourers, craftsmen and merchants. It was not enough simply to proclaim those generous ideals of liberty, equality and fraternity if they did not impact on real life. The old regime had to be replaced with a different system and social hierarchy, a brand-new philosophy and political narrative. This was the purpose of Michelet's analysis of France and its social consciousness, the reason why he became interested in the factors that caused divisions between its various groups.[27]

In his essay *Le Peuple*, Michelet traces these divisions back to the first boom of the capitalist economy. This provides him with more evidence of the interdependence of the disparate sectors of society and the way they collectively contribute to national identity. He argues that France had three social classes before the Revolution, but only two after 1789: the masses and the bourgeoisie. This created the narrative of the class struggle, the conflict between the haves and the have-nots, the division between the bourgeoisie and the proletariat. Other commentators have argued that this view of social class creates a morally loaded polarisation, which characterises one sector as good and the other as evil. The *peuple* are presented as both the victim of an unjust society and a symbol of hope.

Michelet believed that in order for society to become unified the distinction between the self and the other had to dissolve. This was why the proletariat had to sacrifice its own interests for the common good. His ideal community was one that rejected bourgeois self-interest, but did not relinquish the individual rights gained through the Revolution. Similarly to his peers, Michelet was sceptical about the kind of civilisation that might be born out of liberal philosophy. Although he did not go so far as to share the anti-individualist stance of Saint-Simonianism, he was concerned by the excesses of capitalism and felt they were responsible for social division.[28] *Le Peuple* contributed to the antagonism between these groups and its echoes can still be felt nearly two centuries after its conception. It created the bridge between the revolutionary spirit and nationalism. In France, it was adopted and reformulated by the country's many immigrants, who were both attracted and repelled by this ideology.[29]

The working man was at the centre of Michelet's myth of *le peuple*. He represented servitude, but also the willingness to contribute to the state. He embodied poverty, but also camaraderie. Michelet sympathised with this undervalued figure, who for him represented the masses. He was struck by the indifference, apathy and hatred directed towards the poor, hence his own disdainful attack on the commercial world and the *nouveaux riches*. Michelet saw industrialisation as a route to spiritual bankruptcy. Such criticisms reflect an emotional charge in his discourse. It is only because of our ignorance, he claims, that 'we believe we do not need each other'.[30]

The plight of the proletariat touched Michelet deeply, just as it would incense Marx some time later, and he frequently professed his solidarity with this underprivileged group. He anticipated Marx's theories without formulating a unified, dogmatic perspective on the relations between the bourgeoisie and the proletariat. Instead, he focused his attention on understanding the spirit of the masses, of the disenfranchised. Like Victor Hugo, he believed that this marginalised group needed to be seen, heard and understood. He saw the working class as powerless, unable to lift itself out of poverty, yet selflessly dedicated to the common good – a mysterious, peerless force. In contrast, for Marx it represented only a mass of bodies whose prospects were determined by class and their role in the process of production. His abstract and determinist view of society and history meant that he dealt in stereotypes. Michelet, on the contrary, celebrated the solidarity of the working classes, even in the post-industrial era, such as in his descriptions of the squalid outskirts of Paris. Marx, however, saw the lumpen proletariat as forever lost in the 'dark recesses of history'. According to Jacques Julliard, Michelet's sentimental yet rigorous sociological analysis is worlds apart from Marx's political theories.[31]

Michelet's great esteem for the masses meant that he saw them as an embodiment of industriousness, discipline and creativity. Spun out of his imagination, this Romantic myth of the spirit of the common people would enthral the intellectuals and revolutionaries that swarmed to Paris in 1848. While for Herder *das Volk* represented the archetype that had to be resurrected so that Germany might be unified, for Michelet *le peuple* symbolised the attempt to interpret a society in the process of redefining its cultural identity and political institutions. Herder attributed certain behaviours and traditions to the communities he described, just as he insisted on fixed racial characteristics and the purity of the bloodline, all of which allowed him to construct an image of a unique society distinct from any other.[32] Michelet's vision of the ordinary man was less fanciful. He did, however, create a myth that sought to capture the zeitgeist of a new world:

> Without a doubt, *le peuple* understand the world better than we do. Their instinct galvanises both thought and action. Above anything else, it is the essence of spontaneous drive... It defies the absurd dichotomy of instinct and reason which is the curse of our industrial age...[33]

6. LE PEUPLE AND GEOGRAPHICAL DETERMINISM

Michelet not only rejected the idea that the spirit of a nation is tied to issues of race, he also raised questions about the extent to which it is determined by other natural factors. A community develops over time in a particular geographical location. That place becomes 'the homeland', and it would be unreasonable to suggest that geography plays no part in shaping its identity. This locale becomes the site where a community will thrive and forge social bonds. Arguably, geography is more important than racial origins to the formation of nationhood. Nevertheless, Michelet refused to attach too much meaning to geography. His concept of le peuple is born of his Romantic, revolutionary vision, that is, more concerned with the role that the masses will play in the modernisation of France's social and political institutions. One of the consequences of this emancipation was the development of the middle classes. From this perspective, Michelet's peuple appears to be a myth constructed out of necessity rather than mere sentimentality. Although the concept might have had its origins in the past, it was the creation of particular contemporary circumstances: 'Le peuple is a fluid, living concept that crosses boundaries, but has its roots in the ancient earth.'[34]

Yet this did not mean that people were permanently tied to their towns, regions or countries. Reflecting on the history of Ancient Rome, Michelet observed that the relationship between human beings and their natural environment could be described as one of 'harmonious antagonism'. His argument is developed in his writings from 1829 to 1830, when he was teaching at the École Normale. In these texts, he asserts that unlike plants, humans are not bound to the earth, therefore they possess greater freedom to transcend nature, and can move and think as they please. However, despite our independence, our bond with the earth remains.[35]

While for nineteenth-century German historians the connection between land and community was of utmost importance, Michelet's reflections downplay the role of geographical space, hence the difference between his peuple and Volk.[36] In his monograph on Michelet, Paul Viallaneix argues that the revolutionary historian placed humanity neither at the centre of nature nor outside it. In some circumstances, the physical environment, its topography and climate can have substantial impact on human life. Michelet's verdict – based on his philosophical training and analysis of the past – was that this 'harmonious antagonism' was a necessary part of the 'glory of human experience':

> On the one hand we have our humanity, which is defined by its freedom; on the other, we have the immutability of the physical world. The triumph of humanity can be attributed to the fact that we change and adapt, unlike the natural world around us. This is the source of our strength.[37]

Geography played a significant part in Michelet's political ideology and historical narrative, which in turn influenced some of France's most important twentieth-century historians. We sense its importance in his descriptions of the homeland and places with folkloric significance, as well as in the sections from his *Histoire de France*, dedicated to the origin of the concept of *peuple*.

7. THE DISTINGUISHING FEATURES OF MICHELET'S CONCEPT OF PEUPLE

Although it impacted on the formulation of other European ideologies of collective cultural identity, the concept of *peuple* possessed certain distinct qualities of its own. These specific characteristics were formed by France's particular historical and social circumstances in the first half of the nineteenth century. First of all, France had experienced the 1789 revolution, an event that led the country on a journey towards emancipation and modernisation and set it apart from its neighbours. This moment in French history marked the end of the Ancien Régime. In this context, *peuple* emerged as a symbol, a myth through which Michelet conceptualised his political ideology. *Peuple* embodied society, the homeland, the republic, the nation. Michelet laid the foundation for this mythology, and it soon took on different undertones: it captured a society at a moment of change, revealing the conflicts within it, and analysed the consequences of historical events. This 'great spirit' was seen as working towards the improvement of society, shining a light on how its history and culture had shaped it. Such a process would lead to the discovery of common values between its people and the transformation of *peuple* into *nation*. These ideas were outlined in Michelet's essay *Le Peuple* and further developed in his *Histoire de France*, providing a definition of national identity that would influence many historians thereafter. In *Qu'est-ce qu'une Nation?* which we will consider below, Renan also emphasised the notion that 'a nation is a spiritual ideal'. Despite various episodes of political turmoil and the emergence of a new, savage nationalism during the Dreyfus Affair, Michelet's concept of *peuple-nation* stood the test of time. It provided the first sound, coherent definition of French contemporary identity. Michelet's ideology of *peuple* was inherited by numerous French thinkers and slipped into popular discourse just the way he intended.

II

VOLK (PEOPLE) AND SPRACHE (LANGUAGE): HERDER'S THEORIES OF ETHNICITY AND THE NATION

1. FOR A NEW COMPREHENSION OF HERDERIAN IDEOLOGY

The theories of nationhood formulated by Herder and several other intellectuals from the former Austrian Empire need to be revisited for a host of reasons. First of all, it is important to contrast the spiritual dimension, influenced by *Sturm und Drang*, which Hamann, Herder and Goethe brought to this ideology with the more materialist French theories. In addition, we can trace its impact on the public sphere, such as the celebration for the first time of everything that was supposedly German, for example, Gothic art. Such analysis gives us insight into the differences between the French and German cultures in the eighteenth century, including why Diderot's *Encyclopédie*, with its promotion of modern, rational modes of enquiry, did not find favour with contemporary German intellectuals. On the other hand, the analysis of Herderian ideas is important because in this way the speculative theory on collective identity in Central, Eastern and Southeastern Europe could be revised; because the identification of key notions and political languages formed through them is useful to highlight new meritorious aspects of Herder's work, but also to show the lack of discernment contained in his theory of identity.

Herder's writings provide insight into the ideology of national consciousness and the nation state formed around 1800, which remained influential in Central, Eastern and Southeastern Europe during the nineteenth and twentieth centuries. His cultural commentary added a new dimension to the collective ideologies of *Volk* (people) and *Sprache* (language). In attempting to define the character of the nation, Herder leaned more towards the sentimental than the rational. The philosopher Isaiah Berlin described the 'teleological outlook' with reference to German Romanticism. According to this school of thought, individual responsibility is an illusion. As a consequence, despite our best efforts, the process of reasoning 'can never enable us to make completely free choices. Puppets may be conscious and identify themselves happily with the inevitable process in which they play their parts; but it remains inevitable, and they remain marionettes.'[1]

Herder's ideas have been echoed right up to the present day by a number of historians, philosophers, sociologists and linguists concerned with collective identity. He played an important part in the development of German linguistic culture in the nineteenth century. Positivist historiography discusses only the Romantic 'impulse' towards a 'new value system', the 'impetus for scientific study', the treasure trove of southern Slavic proverbs and fairy tales discovered by Herder, Grimm, Schlözer, Müller, Sulzer, Thunmann, Gebhardi and others. It highlights the connection between the cultures of Germany and Eastern Europe and the spiritual influences they exerted on one another. Studies of this kind tend to concentrate all their attention on the ethnography, languages and historical roots of Central, Eastern and Southeastern European countries, but pay no attention to the relationship between culture and political ideology.

Herder's theories paved the way to national and ethnic consciousness. However, considering the intellectual dogmas they promoted by blurring the distinction between reality and fantasy (as seen, for example, in the fictitious, ideologically loaded definition of ethnicity), these theories could be seen as a forerunners to National Socialism and Communism. The academic institutions of Central, Eastern and Southeastern Europe did not focus on regional specificities to enrich their cultural heritage or evaluate their histories objectively, but instead used them to construct the archetype of 'the ethnic being'. These collective identities sprang from their imagination. Essentially, such definitions of identity were based on spiritual and cultural speculations. For these reasons, the genesis of the modern cultural and political identity of Central, Eastern and Southeastern European countries needs to be scrutinised in more detail. The historian Holm Sundhaussen suggests that there are various conflicting elements within it.[2] Moreover, such conflicts may be explained through the analysis of the intellectual history of these countries and its impact on their cultures. Sundhaussen, one of the best-known and most influential German scholars of Southeastern European history, argues that 'The reception of the ideas of Herder and other thinkers by the intelligentsia marks a turn towards a kind of "erudite patriotism" which cannot be put on the same footing as later political nationalism that was fuelled by social and economic factors, although the elements of one were found in the other'.

The realities of many Central and Southeastern European states paint a different picture. For example, in Poland, Hungary, Romania, Bulgaria, Yugoslavia and Albania it was these same social and cultural discrepancies that had an impact on economic history and political thought in the middle of the nineteenth century, as well as much later. Nationalism has been and remains linked to the way in which the intellectual elite has managed the social, professional, religious and linguistic diversity within the states in question. That is, the nation and nationalism did not appear as an internal necessity, but as a result of the cultivation of differences or the rejection of the 'other'. In other words, nationalism asserted itself by appealing to the majority and discriminating against the disadvantaged on the basis of education, wealth, political rights, language, religion, origins and number.

Scholars such as Ştefan Stratimirović, Vuk Karadzič, Dositej Obradović, Sándor Farkas Bölönyi, István Széchenyi, Ioan Maiorescu, Simion Bărnuţiu, A. T. Laurian, Alexandru Papiu Ilarian, Vasile Conta, A. C. Popovici and others, not to mention countless other Serbian, Hungarian and Romanian writers, have all been inspired by the Herderian theory of the nation.[3] Across the region, a preoccupation with the uniqueness of their own community led to the exaggeration of differences of any kind of minorities and provoked a nationalism that was fed to the masses through propaganda, with the purpose of conquering and preserving the power of a privileged group. Monoculturalism became the ideal, although the whole area we are referring to is characterised by multiculturalism and a wide range of ethnic hybrids as well as cultural ambiguities. The diversity and convergence of diversity as a way of generating identities with multiple linguistic, cultural and ethnographic roots were natural in the spaces administered by the two great empires that ruled Central and Southeastern Europe: the Hapsburg Empire and the Ottoman Empire.

In fact, this intelligentsia, intent on promoting differentialism and ethnic nationalism, adapted the theories of Herder and his peers to their own interests. It was only the privileged group in society that was encouraged to foster its identity. The heirs of aristocratic families as well as many members of the Central, Eastern and Southeastern European intellectual elites adopted the Herderian ethnonational idea in order to preserve the power of their clans. This did not aid the implementation of modern values or create stability for all individuals in society. Instead, it created an obstacle to overcoming economic backwardness, poverty and corruption. A certain hierarchy inherited from the medieval world dominated social relations (and, in some cases, still dominates them). Nationalism in these areas could never be accurately described as 'erudite patriotism' despite claims to the contrary.

The reduction of national culture to the single component of ethnicity fails to engage with the social and political context of the past. Instead, by formulating a definition of identity solely on this basis, we create imaginary connections between the past and the present. These cultural ideologies give rise to political myths. The parallel discourse of the Western and Central, Eastern and Southeastern European philosophers is the result of two schools of thought: one that prioritises *jus soli* and another that reverts to *jus sanguinis*. German historians tend to ignore the connotations of *Volk* and *Sprache* – as Herder defines them – or, in other words, the political and cultural mix that clearly contributed to the genesis of these differentialist ideologies.

The disparity between the entities concerned with ethnoculturalism and those interested in building social and civic institutions demonstrates the different identities established in those two parts of Europe. For this reason we must re-examine Herder's theories and their impact on the eastern part of the continent, from the nineteenth century to the present.

The intellectuals of Central, Eastern and Southeastern Europe had a vested interest, and this antagonism to diversity led to social fragmentation and interfaith and interethnic conflicts. There are many opposing aspirations and ideological positions that must be taken into account when examining the problems of Romania, the former Yugoslavia and Albania, or when identifying the cultural and political phenomena of twentieth-century Hungary, marked as it is by the existence of several million native speakers of Hungarian outside the borders of their own nation state. As such, Herderianism laid new ground and stimulated a collective narcissism as well as the military, strategic and economic interests of Prussia and Bismarck's Germany with regard to their Eastern neighbours, although its positive contributions, such as the identification of specific idiolects and ethnography, hide a much more complex reality. Being more poetic than pragmatic, this ethnonationalism which was developed on the basis of the Herderian concept of collective identity failed to provoke the expected break from the medieval era and to encourage the modernisation of societies. The first emancipation arguably took place during the eighteenth-century administration of the Turks, when the Phanariot families played an important role in the first process of modernisation of the Danube Principalities, and it was also accelerated by the Enlightenment policies of the Hapsburgs.

Language, too, played a primary role in Herder's philosophy, providing the very foundations of his doctrine. He describes how it might be used to express states of consciousness as well as to define our external reality. Unlike his predecessors, Herder believed that consciousness derived from the soul and that language derived from these spiritual values. The ability to reflect and meditate is rooted in people's spiritual strength. In this way, humans construct a clear image through their senses – Herder was always wedded to this idea – and identify certain distinctive elements which they can then begin to define. Language is the first product of our consciousness. Thanks to this process, Herder argues, 'human language is conceived'.[4] The discovery of words is based on people's ability to perceive sounds as memorable signs that reflect their understanding of the exterior world. Human beings are creatures who listen and remember. They not only use language – their consciousness is created by language.

If, for example, a person found themselves on a desert island, they would recognise the sounds of nature through their soul 'which is never entirely mute', and their other senses would detect the movements of the water, the wind and the animals, thus demonstrating the indissoluble link between language, thought and instinct. Herder was so convinced by his theory that he saw the senses as informing language and mental processes: 'Let each man's senses be free... to feel all the creatures that address his hearing.' Divine nature, he argued, would enable man to find his voice, and for this reason Herder regarded it as his Muse.

Overall, the 'erudite patriotism' inspired by Herder's ideas had a much less significant effect. Unlike Holm Sundhaussen, I would argue that there is a close connection between Herder's late eighteenth-century concept of the nation and later political nationalism. The emphasis on ethnographic, linguistic and cultural differences, as well as the categorical assertion of a so-called 'right of blood', were ideas formulated by Herder that inspired and fuelled 'erudite patriotism', and later led to intolerant ethnonationalism, as we will see in Chapter IV below.

2. THE 'GENIUS' OF *STURM UND DRANG*

Herder believed that humans 'invented' speech from natural sounds, hence his theory that these are signs recalled from the inner consciousness. In this way he suggested that language is not simply a means of communication, but also the original creation of an ethnic culture. Many great poets, writers and academics have explored the relationship between *Volk* and *Sprache*. It was regarded as the first step towards identifying all that is unique and specific to every sociocultural entity: 'Critics, learn your language and strive to prepare it for poetry, philosophy and prose.' Why? Because this is the only way to learn to think, the only way to marry the genius of language with the genius of a nation's literature. What does genius mean to Herder and his contemporaries? According to the *Sturm und Drang* generation, the notion of 'genius' referred to a state of mind, a way of theorising and a heightened individualism. For the irrationalist Hamann, the term 'genius' meant an inexplicable mysterious force, comparable only to religious faith. For Herder, genius was the source of all discovery and human creation.

Language is central to the literature of *Volk*. Herder's writing is filled with allusions intended to create an emotional connection with the reader's soul: 'You have to represent artificially the natural expression of feeling, as a cube is projected on a flat surface; you have to express the whole tone of feeling in the periods, in the disposition and the connection between the words...'[5] The passage continues in a similar vein, favouring metaphors rather than clear explanations. The significance of language in Herder's theories reflects his political views. Our mother tongue allows us the broadest perspective on the world, he writes. Eloquence guarantees that human 'boldness' will not turn into 'iniquity':

[Language] was imprinted on us in the most tender years, when the power of words allowed our soul to embrace a world of notions and images that later transforms into the poet's treasure. In the mother tongue [man] can reason and express himself with perfect ease, the poet can discover a wealth of images and colours, for we see in this language the flash of lightning hurled down by the gods and it is the place from which our thoughts and spirit grow. How could I ever express myself better than in my mother tongue? To the one who was the child of her heart, the baby she carried on her breast, the branch she raised in her hands, she is more charming than any other language and she is as precious as the homeland, bringing joy to our best years and surviving, full of hope and honour, through the ages...[6]

This passage implies that identity is defined through language and that this language is connected to the homeland. Language, Herder argued, raises people out of barbarism. He believed that the populations on which a foreign language – Latin – had been imposed for almost a millennium did not progress at the same rate as other communities. Herder argued that, as a result, these groups lacked national monuments and local laws that would ensure effective, independent governments and preserve 'national history'. As Sundhaussen pointed out, this was more than just a matter of social identity. The concepts of *Volk* and *Sprache* were viewed by Herder as creating a cultural identity that turned away from barbarism, forming a collective capable of understanding itself and aware of its own characteristics. The Romantic was not concerned with the self as an individual, but with its role within a community that was undergoing a constant evolution. Language was understood as the engine of historical development rather than simply a tool of understanding, as a metaphor rather than a formative element of thought.

Herder's sentimentality mirrors the spirit of the *Sturm und Drang* era, according to which the inception of the peoples-nations sprang from their ethnographic and cultural heritages. Language was to be the fastest and most effective means of consolidating the interests of society, but above all it was to reveal political conflicts. By placing such emphasis on the significance of the mother tongue, which Herder perceived as the foundation of every cultural good, he promoted the idea that a community should seek a deeper understanding of itself. In this light, language becomes the materialisation of the soul of the people and their character, thus implying an inextricable tie between ethnic heritage and national consciousness.[7] Absolute truth lies in the memory and the imagination, while spiritual insight establishes cohesion.

Herder wrote that 'Fantasy flies up, self-awareness spreads its wings, all expressions of one and the same energy and litheness of the soul', concluding that the inner life and spiritual enlightenment are built on speech. Like Hegel, Herder assumed that people and societies were part of a larger, spiritual realm. Contemporary history, literature, philosophy and historiography written in this register invented structures, discovered specificities and described people's actions and spiritual motivations, forming a basis for explaining the existence of the ethnonation and genesis of the nation state. This is how teleology, one of the metaphysical branches of history, was born. All these arguments were based on the ideas promoted by the spirit of *Sturm und Drang*, and they added a revolutionary dimension to the concept of the ethnonation in the nineteenth century. The reflections of Herder's generation are suffused with spirituality. Herder's ideal, like Hamann's, is characterised by a return to origins, the celebration of specific traditions, an emphasis on historical evolution or historical continuity and the revelation of the divine plan of humanity. In *Philosophy of History* (1773) he asserts that civilisations develop as living organisms, moving from childhood towards maturity and old age. This implies that historical evolution is cyclical, which seems incredible from a scientific perspective.

But for Herder the Romantic historian, logic was not a priority. He believed that sensibility surpassed anything else. He sought to ignite the reader's imagination with a display of metaphors. For example, he claims that the decline of poetry was due to the fact that 'expression turned into mere artifice' and 'stole' the lyricism of nature. Ideas could not be separated from modes of expression. Regarding Herder's prose, Kant commented that such passages reflect a predilection for analogies and highlight an imagination that tends to mobilise emotions and passions in order to express the essence of a subject steeped in mystery. The emotional force behind these speculations makes them seem more profound, so that we interpret them as 'allusions with deep meanings', and in this way reality is replaced by fiction. Synonyms will pass as explanations and allegories as truths, making rational analysis impossible. Kant, the last and most important figure of the Enlightenment, was perplexed by this language, considering it incomprehensible. He was the first to criticise Herder's theoretical speculations, noting how the critical analysis and scientific knowledge of the Enlightenment were being overturned. Herder, Hamann and Fichte had replaced it with teleological thinking, aspiring to invent new ways of interpreting human evolution and its relationship with nature.

Undoubtedly, there was a political motivation to Herder's definition of ethnoculture. The imagined ideal of Germany depended on the unified consciousness of German-language speakers. Therefore, these theories were intended to stimulate actions that would produce a new social and political order; their purpose was not only to stir emotions, but to revive and propagate the national spirit. There was a fundamental difference between Herder's and Michelet's intentions; between the concepts of *Volk* and *peuple*; between the German *Kulturnation* that placed the organic being in the foreground and the French *nation* that sought to create a consciousness shared by all members of society. For example, Ernest Renan's analysis of Herder's work and his references to national identity – like that of other historians who pointed out differences between the German and French ideologies – is meaningless, as it eschews a real comparative perspective that facilitates the understanding of identity theories. Herder was not discouraged by the obstacles that his German Muse would encounter: 'We walk slowly, but confidently; we do not hurry, but take the best route towards our goal, which is in sight.'

3. 'SONGS ARE THE PEOPLE'S ARCHIVE' – PRUSSIA'S GERMAN ASPIRATIONS, EMBODIED BY *KULTURNATION*

This tension between poetry and politics resulted in a call to action as soon as its people realised the urgency of their mission: 'Germany must feel what action means…' Otherwise, this would only be possible if the people became aware of the importance of action. 'In the interim it is good for the people to sing their nation's songs and wait for the time of nature and its action. Songs are the people's archive… [and through them] peoples define themselves.'[8] Herder believed these songs were the key to ethnic origins. In fact, his interest in folk music was neither arbitrary nor motivated simply by a desire for cultural emancipation. Herder's thought centred on a *Kulturnation*, a cultural nation represented by a *Volk*, a community that was distinct in its language and history. His texts did not merely aim to take stock of ideas, but also to uncover the relation between language and thought and to construct myths. By combining findings from various disciplines, he formulated a theory that would give his readers an appetite for history. Based on these ideas, the genesis of German aspirations in Prussia became possible. Imagination went as far as to promote radical distinctions in the pedagogy of the ethnonation.

The new wave of bold, outspoken politicians decried the existence of independent principalities inherited from the medieval age, regarding them as a privileged space for the assertion of civil society and the urban bourgeoisie. Herder had anticipated their concerns and recommended ways of reviving these institutions. Like Hegel, he identified with the forces that fought for change and reflected the heightened passions of his era. It is worth noting that this change had little in common with the English liberal ideal or British nationalist aspirations at any point in history. Nor was the spirit of post-Revolutionary and post-Napoleonic France – where the Congress of Vienna and the Holy Alliance had promised to stabilise social and political life – fully reflected in the philosophies of Herder and his contemporaries. The different historical contexts resulted in alternative forms of discourse. The German and French Romantics had their own particular definitions of emancipation. Herder was convinced that his theories should be embraced by all who fought for the advancement of mankind. For him, progress amounted to a seismic change within Prussian-German culture:

> Of course, Germany will not have a Homer, as he could only sing of his enslaved brothers, defeated in America, and we could not expect a Tyrtaeus to lead its armies...[9] The harp will fall silent and dissolve in fog as long as religion, the interests of the people and the homeland are so divided, burdened, starved of light. But keep faith, poor, broken Germany, trampled underfoot! The end of your misfortune is in sight. The spirit of the nation will henceforth be your bard and love will breed among your sons because we have come so far and conquered many obstacles under the banner of truth, religion, simplicity, as even our enemies would not dare deny. We will clear the way, keep our eyes fixed on the goal and we will reach it, through our people's will.[10]

The purpose of this impassioned prose was to win hearts and minds and transform the significance of language in the social sphere. It sought to stir the collective unconscious by persuading the population that they were part of a significant historical moment. There are references in this passage to Romantic themes such as truth, religion and simplicity, but it also reveals the writer's attitudes towards race, nation and class. The tone is characteristic of the determinist philosophy which defined the German spirit, and its aim was to unite the entire German-speaking population. Herder's invention of a fictive ethnicity laid the foundations of the ethnonation. His approach is typical of a certain Romantic idealistic monism. According to Herder, poetry was the only authentic way of discovering truth, as it filled the soul with a 'sweet inclination'. It was this truth that he wanted the whole nation to embrace, but this would only be possible when society was completely unified. While the intellectual elite had grappled with these issues for centuries, the poet alone had the power to drive people's hearts in the right direction and make them strive for those ideals. According to Herder, the poet was a deity and an inspirational leader:

> But he who knows the worth of his noble talent, who loves his people and brethren, who escapes the quagmire of lassitude and the clutches of the perverts and the sodomites, he who aspires to the nobility of Orpheus and Homer, or even strives to become another prophet, a Moses, bending his ear to the voice of nature and truth, catching the spark of creative power and love that has fallen from heaven and lives in every poet, that chosen one who speaks the deepest truth of his heart – how he will touch the souls of everyone who listens to his message and lead them towards their destiny! And yet he is a mere vessel through which the real treasure shines, he is the iron bound to the magnet through whom bright sparks of energy shall flow... Such is the way that divine poetry electrifies people and nations. But why do I waste my breath speaking about this wondrous art when instead I should fall silent and submit to its force?[11]

Herder's perspective on the world contrasted with that of his French counterparts. His ideal modes of speech, thought and behaviour were inspired by the spirit of the Middle Ages. According to Herder, the poet was 'the chosen one', a superior being destined to convey this sublime message to the masses by capturing their souls, his genius giving him access to nature's 'greatest and most profound' mysteries. For him, the nation was created by poets and only poetry could sanctify it with its 'truth', 'simplicity' and 'divine purity'. There is an implicit criticism here of the materialist doctrines of French scholars from the 1789 revolution.

Herder's concept of the ethnonation was bound up with ideas about nature, the spark of inspiration, omnipotence and omnipresence, all of which surpassed the actions of ordinary individuals within society. Instead, the fate of the community lay in the hands of an intellectual and artistic elite. The Romantic historian's fantasy of this ideal nation relied on the emergence of great poets who would be able to bring forth that century-old ideal.

Volk required a special leader to channel its energies in the right direction and realise its ideals. Herder saw himself as a bard of the people, able to ignite the 'electric spark' that would create socio-political change. In his writings, he tends to ignore the differences between various regions clustered around the Rhine, the Oder and the Danube. His brand of 'fictive ethnicity' would become a model for most German-speaking philosophers of the nineteenth century. It was disseminated via certain history books espousing ethnonationalist ideologies that began to influence the intellectual elites of neighbouring regions even before these became fully fledged political states. Amid this backdrop, the concept of the nation state was overshadowed by the idea of an organic nation. The *Volk* as a tribe, community or organic collective being had become the new ideal of nationhood.

Where did Herder's interest in the ethnic roots of the nation originate? And was his antipathy towards the eighteenth-century French political culture that had emerged after the 1789 revolution justified? What were his objections to Voltaire's theories and why did he come to reject Kant's philosophy? Herderianism exerted an influence not only in Germany, but also across Central, Eastern and Southeastern Europe. Herder saw himself as a great visionary, heralding a new modern age in which his society would be reorganised under the banner of *Volk*. Influenced by the theories of Fichte and Hegel and borrowing the discourse of mystical metaphysics, he formulated the ideals of the 'heroic man' and the 'heroic life' as part of a quest to fulfil his nation's destiny. Herder saw himself as the messenger of the spirit of the people, but his language games created a closed universe reminiscent of Leibniz's monads:[12]

> But feeling, motion, action – even if they should prove inconsequential (for what has timeless consequence on the stage of mankind?), if there will be knocks and revolutions, if these feelings will at times turn fanatical, violent, even detestable – as instruments in the hands of time, how great their power and effect! How they nourish the heart, not the head! How they bind everything together with inclinations and

drives, not with sickly thoughts – reverence and the honour of knights, boldness in love and civic strength, constitution and legislation, religion! Nothing could be further from my mind than to defend the endless mass-migrations and devastations, the vassals' wars and feuds, the armies of monks, the pilgrimages and crusades: I only wish to explain them, to show how spirit breathes in everything, after all! The fermentation of human forces, the great cure of the whole species by forced movement, and, if I may speak so boldly, Fortune's rewinding of the great wound-down clock – albeit with great clamour and the inevitable disruption of the weights' calm repose! So the wheels rattled![13]

Herder's opinions were inspired by the spirit of the *Sturm und Drang* movement, whose influence was felt throughout Europe during the Enlightenment. Prussia's political structures diverged from those of France or the Hapsburg Empire. There was no such thing as a unified Germany at the end of the eighteenth century. Napoleon's political impact was felt only after 1800. So where did Herder's plan for the reorganisation of German society come from?

A close examination of the passage above reveals that Herder is in favour of wars, seeing them as fuelled by spirit and passion. By decreeing that 'violent' eruptions are a form of 'catharsis' for humankind, Herder blurs the boundary between good and evil. His argument that exalted feelings and violence are sources of human power suggests that he feels that reason plays no part in human actions. Herder places the constitution and legislation in relation to piety, religion and chivalric honour. The writer-philosopher acknowledges that he sees history as a perpetual struggle. His references to the origins of mankind or to the great cultures of antiquity mirror his aspirations for his own community. In fact, it was an attempt to create a point of reference through which to understand contemporary events. Commenting on this philosophy of history, Elias Palti argues that although the idea of a divine, mysterious plan was first conceived in Herder's theory, the concept of the power of 'man in general' can be traced back to the Enlightenment. Herder emphasised the specificity of each cultural and national community, and in doing so he became a founder of modern historicism. His writings reflect two main concerns: the relationship between humanity and nature and the tension between instinct and rationality.

4. THE SPIRIT OF THE PEOPLE, VIEWED FROM A SCIENTIFIC PERSPECTIVE

> It is obvious that human life, as far as it is vegetation, has the fate of plants. As these, so man and animals are produced from seed, which too, like the germ of a future tree, requires a matrix. Plant-like its first form is developed in the womb; and, out of it, does not the structure of our fibres, in their first buds and powers, nearly resemble that of the fibres of the sensitive plant? Our ages too are the ages of a plant: we spring up, grow, bloom, wither and die. We are called forth without our consent: no one is asked of what sex he will be; from what parents he will descend; on what spot he will be born to poverty or wealth; or by what internal or external cause he will at last be brought to his end.[14]

Herder believed that, like every other creature, humans are part of nature and should 'obey its great laws'. He regarded nature as the source of life that endows humans with 'all its powers'. By studying the latest discoveries in the natural sciences, he began to construct a new conception of humanity. He summarised the distinctions or parallels between humans and animals as follows:

> The young of the human species comes into the world weaker than that of any other animal, and for an obvious reason: because it is formed to receive a figure that cannot be fashioned in the womb... The feeble child, therefore, is an invalid, as I may say, in its superior powers, and Nature is earliest improving these, and continues incessantly to improve them. Before the child learns to walk, it learns to see, to hear, to feel, and to practise the delicate mechanism and geometry of these senses. It exercises these in the same instinctive manner as the brute, only in a nicer degree...
> Man with his erect posture acquired a delicacy, warmth and

strength that no brute can attain. In the savage state he was in great measure covered with hair, particularly on the back; and for the deprivation of this coat the elder Pliny has loudly complained against Nature. The benevolent mother of all has given man a more beautiful covering in his skin, which, with all its delicacy, is capable of supporting the changes of season and the temperature of every climate, when aided by a small portion of art, which to him is second nature.

To this art he is led not solely by naked necessity, but by something more lovely and more appropriate to man. Whatever some philosophers may assert, modesty is natural to the human species; and indeed something bearing an obscure analogy to it is so to a few of the brutes...[15]

Although these descriptions are redolent of contemporary botanical or anatomical treatises, they also reflect a Romantic perspective. There is no discussion here about the value of education or human relationships, both of which were tropes of the eighteenth century. Humanity is instead defined solely through its relationship with nature, which is cast as the source of its strength and vitality. 'When Nature exalted man,' says Herder, 'she made him the ruler of the earth. His upright position gave him a finer construction, a more refined circulatory system, a more diverse mixture of vital fluids and, as a result, a greater ability to moderate bodily temperature, thanks to which he was able to survive in both Siberia and Africa.' Evidently, Herder considered that man's innate power was generated by his genetic makeup. This view – outlined in his best-known and most widely read books, such as *Ideen zur Philosophie der Geschichte der Menschheit* (*Reflections on the Philosophy of the History of Mankind*) – was influenced by biological theory:

The genetic power is the mother of all the forms upon Earth, climate acting merely as an auxiliary or antagonist. How must the man have been astonished, who first saw the wonders of the creation of a living being! Globules, with fluids shooting between them, become a living point; and from this point an animal forms itself. The heart soon becomes visible and, weak and imperfect as it is, begins to beat; the blood, which existed before the heart, begins to redden; soon the head appears;

soon eyes, a mouth, the senses and limbs display themselves. Still there is no breast, yet there is a motion in the internal parts; there are no bowels, yet the animal opens its mouth. The little brain is not yet enclosed in the head, or the heart in the breast; the ribs and bones are like a spider's web; but quickly the wings, feet, toes, hips appear, and the living creature receives more nourishment... What would he who saw this wonder for the first time call it? There, he would say, is a *living organic power*: I know not whence it came, or what it intrinsically is; but that it is there, that it lives, that it has acquired itself organic parts out of the chaos of homogeneal matter, I see – this is incontestable.[16]

Where did Herder's fascination with anatomy and morphology come from? Typically, his discourse understates the role of rationality in human life. Instead, he prefers to discuss the influence of genetics, seeing it as the 'organic' source of human life and power. After all, he argues, only a healthy body can host a thriving spiritual life. The soul cannot be divided from the 'animal heat' of our physical beings, and nature controls all our actions. Thoughts are themselves 'organic', and this is the very reason why man is the most perfect creature of all: 'Human perfection is shaped by subtle organic forces which created intricate structures.' With this argument, Herder concludes that humans are essentially different from one another as their characteristics are moulded by their environment, in the same way that animals and plants adapt to their habitat.

The natural sciences provided Herder with the type of evidence that supported his own outlook on the world and allowed him to formulate his theories. Using this information, he intended to show that each person and each era perceives itself as the centre of history. He was convinced that in order to understand history, we must focus on 'genetics'.[17] Following on from his reflections on the idea of the species, Herder began to form the notion of 'national character'. Applying biological theories to human communities, he argued that the customs of our ancestors are passed down through history and mould the behaviour of descendants who inherit the same distinctive character traits. In this way, the ancestors become the prototype of the species. Herder cites the Jews as evidence of a people whose particular characteristics have been passed on through generations. Such speculations form the basis of his myth of national character. Herder asserted that the Jews retained these characteristics everywhere they lived, even as they mixed with Egyptians, Chinese, Arabs or Hindus. According to him, this national distinctness has survived from the ancient world into the modern era. He considered that those states that had remained independent and true to their roots had fared better than those engulfed by empires, as they had not suffered the same oppression, frustration and unrest. Such states 'may be subjugated, but their national spirit continues to exist'. Herder saw monocultural identity as the ultimate ideal:

> Thus it is with China: we well know how much labour it cost its conquerors to introduce there a simple custom, the Mongol mode of cutting the hair. Thus it is with the Brahmins and Jews, whose ceremonial systems will eternally separate them from all the nations upon Earth. Thus Egypt long withstood any intermixture with other nations: and how difficult was it to extirpate the Phoenicians, merely because they were a people rooted in this spot!...
>
> Hence we may infer the reason why ancient political constitutions laid so much stress on the formation of manners by education: as their internal strength depended wholly on this spring. Modern kingdoms are built on money or mechanical politics; the ancient, on the general way of thinking of a nation from its infancy; and as nothing has a more efficacious influence upon children than religion, most of the ancient states, particularly those of Asia, were more or less theocratic. I know the aversion in which this name is held, as to it all the evil that has at any time oppressed mankind is in great measure ascribed. Its abuses I will by no means undertake to defend; but at the same time it is true that this form of government is not only adapted to the infancy of the human race, but necessary to it: otherwise, assuredly, it would neither have extended so far, nor have maintained itself so long.[18]

The ultimate intent of Herder's historical analysis is clear. His desire to conserve the past and connect people with their origins, coupled with his emphasis on the importance of religion and its significance to the roots of humankind, fits perfectly within his philosophy. His writings create connections between all the elements that bind people to their ancestors.

Herder adds the example of the Greeks to those of the Jews and the Egyptians. He draws a clear outline of the evolution of Hellenic history and refers back to zoological and botanical theories in his explanation of how the migration of its people from one area to another did not attenuate their typical characteristics, but intensified them: 'The same seeds might thrive better when they are planted in new soil and produce healthier, hardier plants.' In this passage, as in many others, Herder refers to the movement of the German people from Asia to Europe. His book *Geist der Völker* (*Spirit of Peoples*) attempts to define German identity and put it at the centre of the community's consciousness.[19] Herder's political theories are largely concerned with tracing the origins of various groups and their distinguishing characteristics, working towards the conclusion that their education and way of thinking are determined by their genetics. From this, he surmises that the spirit of a people is the product of its unique language, soul and mode of experiencing the world. The science, religion, spirituality, history, joys and sufferings of every nation are reflected in its current way of life.

Herder's philosophical generalisations are intended to paint a new, prophetic vision of society:

> The natural state of man is society: for in this he is born and brought up; to this he is led by the awakening propensities of his youth; and the most pleasing appellations of father, son, brother, sister, lover, friend are ties of the law of Nature, that exist in every primitive society of men. On these too the first governments have been founded: family regulations, without which the species could not subsist; laws, that Nature gave, and sufficiently limited.[20]

In Herder's philosophy, nature plays a central role as it determines all social and national characteristics – the area of greatest interest to him, which he investigates using the methodology of the natural sciences. His theories lead him to assert that a nation can only be composed of a single people, and that empires fail because they cannot integrate disparate communities that possess their own individual characters. Such empires are unnatural because they bring together communities that can thrive only if they are separate entities. The importance of blood ties plays a significant role in his argument, as they bring people together into a cohesive group:

> Nature educates families; the most natural state therefore is *one* nation, with one national character. This it retains for ages, and this is most naturally formed when it is the object of its native princes: for a nation is as much a natural plant as a family, only with more branches. Nothing therefore appears so directly opposite to the ends of government as the unnatural enlargement of states, the wild mixture of various races and nations under one sceptre. A human sceptre is far too weak and slender for such incongruous parts to be engrafted upon it: glued together indeed they may be into a fragile machine, termed a machine of state, but destitute of internal vivification and sympathy of parts. Kingdoms of this kind, which render the name of fathers of their country scarcely applicable to the best of potentates, appear in history like that type of monarchies in the vision of the prophet, where the lion's head, the dragon's tail, the eagle's wings and the paws of a bear combined in one unpatriotic figure of a state. Such machines are pieced together like the Trojan horse; guaranteeing one another's immortality though destitute of national character, there is no life in them, and nothing but the curse of Fate can condemn to immortality the forced union: for the very politics that framed them are those that play with men and nations as with inanimate substances. But history sufficiently shows that these instruments of human pride are formed of clay, and like all other clay, will dissolve or crumble to pieces.[21]

For Herder, the political state can be understood only in relation to the ethnic origins of its people, and as a result he disparages the empires that controlled the regions surrounding Prussia. Herder's image of the nation was that of a plant, and its root was the vernacular of its people. He criticised the Hapsburg Empire as he rejected the idea of a multicultural state. Nevertheless, he was an acute observer of developments in contemporary political life, and his theories reflect this keen interest. His objections to the Hapsburg Empire's subjugation of a multicultural community and its reformist ideology rooted in the Enlightenment can be traced back to his *Sturm und Drang* notion that 'the most natural state' was the state composed of 'only one people'. Herder's faith lay in the people rather than the state, believing that their inherent characteristics could never be destroyed by time or space. For him, *Volk* is eternal, while political states prosper, then dissolve. His Romantic perspective urges the state to nurture the bonds between its people, to utilise their toil and intelligence, to harness their energy and channel it towards the highest goal – 'the common good'. To challenge this enterprise, he seems to say, is to defy the laws of nature.

5. THE PURITY OF *VOLK* AND THE ORGANIC NATION

Herder dreamt of a Germany that would become an ethnonation and, by extension, of a Europe formed of ethnonations that would cultivate their own distinct identities based on their languages, traditions, intellectual history and origins: 'I admire any nation that, like our Germany, fans the flames of the community spirit and shines like a beacon of inspiration for others.'[22] Any form of cultural appropriation is perceived as dangerous, as it detracts from the highest goal – the preservation of a people's natural characteristics. Herder's *Volk* purism was associated with linguistic purism, its main role being to bring to the forefront differentiating characteristics: 'Have you ever considered the effect of a Franco-German education? For the Germans, it is a dry and hollow experience.'[23] Language, as Herder saw it, was intended to cultivate the deepest feelings of the German spirit, and therefore a French education would only prove an unfortunate distraction. He was alluding here to the behaviour of Berlin intellectuals during the Enlightenment years, when French became not only the preferred language of the royalty, but was also adopted by Prussian burghers and aristocrats.[24] Herder argues for returning to the roots of German culture. His zeal inflames him to propose radical solutions on how the doctrine of the ethnonation should be communicated to the people. He believed that patriotism required a purge: everything foreign or contaminated by contact with the 'other' had to be rejected. The ethnonation should not be judged by how it was seen by others, only by its self-image:

> I feel nothing but contempt and disgust when I see the leaders of certain countries meddling in the business of other nations and disturbing their harmonious ways of life... Every country should respect its neighbours' boundaries and autonomy, otherwise they are undermining their national identity. When we cross that line, everything is lost.[25]

Is this the precursor of a theory of race? Unlike Hegel, Herder did not draw a clear, systematic connection between the people's spirit and their blood.[26] His work, which served as the foundation of an era of nationalism, cannot be ignored or taken lightly as it popularised the theory of the ethnonation. While Hegel does not give us a perspective on history but rather a personal view of its development, Herder goes to great pains to convey his outlook on the significance of the species in relation to political thought. But Herder's essentialism is itself not historical. Nevertheless, the concept of *Volksgeist* derived from Leibniz's theory of monads proved very attractive to a number of intellectuals. Herder's original contribution was his application of biological theory to history. He combines *Volksgeist* with the concept of vitalism, thus giving it spiritual undertones and attempting to find the overarching significance of human evolution. Herder's conclusions, which became a point of interest for a whole host of nineteenth-century academics, included the idea that developments in human history were orchestrated by a supernatural force. Only divine intervention could breathe life into matter.

Elias Palti questions the basis of Herder's radical interpretation of history.[27] As well as being a reaction to the Enlightenment, Herder's philosophy was influenced by the natural sciences and can be placed somewhere between the concepts of *fulguratio* and *evolutio*. Herderian vitalism explicitly deals with two Enlightenment concerns: the genetic inheritance of a new creature and its subsequent development. Later, Herder – like many thinkers in the first half of the nineteenth century – became intrigued by one particular dilemma: how can we introduce a dynamic component into the original matrix of consciousness, which excludes every transformative idea, without calling on mysterious and supernatural powers?

Herder's theories quickly gained notoriety in the German-speaking world. His books were relatively easy to translate and soon spread throughout revolutionary Europe. They became particularly popular with Czech, Hungarian, Romanian, Serbian and Greek academics. *Ideen zur Philosophie der Geschichte der Menschheit* was celebrated for its spirited, poetic style which won much admiration for its author. In France, Quinet translated *Ideen* and echoed some of Herder's theories in his own writings. In Hungary, he was admired by István Széchenyi and in Transylvania by Gheorghe Barițiu and Ioan Maiorescu. Mihail Kogălniceanu read him in Moldova, and in Wallachia he exerted an influence on the revolutionary Nicolae Bălcescu. Herderianism became a reference point for all academics and ideologues concerned with ethnic differentialism, and was used as the basis of their ethnonationalist doctrines. In practice, this promoted the interests of the feudal aristocracy who paid lip service to modernisation. Collectivity remained a fiction, as the privileged (with a few notable exceptions) used the propaganda of ethnoculture to retain their power. Although seeming to emulate the German cultural and political model, the elites of Central, Eastern and Southeastern Europe facilitated only a limited form of emancipation, as their main priority was to protect their own privileges. Due to the backwardness of the masses living in those regions, *Volksgeist* never achieved the same liberal goals as it had in Western Europe.

Ernest Renan's political theories reveal the consequences of the ideology of the 'organic nation'. According to Renan, there is something evil in political ideology based on this perception of nature, and he considers it the seed that subsequently grew into wars. To argue that this concept of the nation – which Renan described as 'a daily plebiscite' – was not useful to the peoples within the Hapsburg Empire as, according to Holm Sundhaussen, it did not acknowledge their right to political change, is to ignore the socio-economic and cultural-political disadvantages of those regions. It also underestimates the enormous impact of *Sturm und Drang* and the powerful way its ideas resonated in the regions east and south of Vienna.

As the ideologies of Herder and his supporters spread through the empire, they created an appetite for emancipation and differentialism. The empire, caught unprepared for these challenges, began to lose its absolute authority. Even some of its own leaders had been seduced by the ideas of *Volksgeist* and *Kulturnation*, and this led to a political culture based on irrationality, namely an atmosphere of conflict between groups of people who had lived together side by side harmoniously for hundreds of years: this was the mentality that instigated civil wars and endless disputes over territory, origins, history and language. Renan's criticism of the theory of the 'organic nation' (the ethnonation) posed a direct challenge to Herder. The fact that the intellectuals of the Hapsburg Empire were not able to distinguish between these theorists' positions could be explained by the fact that they had been educated in German, but this confusion led to the gradual undermining of the imperial structures. At the same time, this example shows that Prussia, and later Germany, would become the main external competitor of the Hapsburgs in the occupation and domination of Central, Eastern and Southeastern Europe. Finally, the most eminent intellectuals in Central, Eastern and Southeastern Europe did not enjoy an audience prepared for either of these theories of national identity, hence they adopted the elitist position.

In the eighteenth and nineteenth centuries there was a growing interest in the history of ideas. The term that best encapsulated this was *Begriffsgeschichte*, which was apparently first coined by Hegel and reflected the long history of this fascination with the origins of languages and lexicography. The Romantics and Enlightenment thinkers immersed themselves in every discipline, but particularly favoured historiography and philology. The results of their enquiries were limited, however, and of little use to modern social scientists. For this reason, we must subject them to a hermeneutic study, focusing on key words and concepts, some of which became very influential, to reconsider their historical meaning. The modern researcher has the advantage of using advanced methodology that places language and social interests at the heart of interpreting historical events.

Herder's neglect of social factors reflected his apparent ignorance of Locke's and Montesquieu's ideas about the nature of political institutions. His notions of history and collective identity were based on the evolution of society and the significance of language.[28] Passages from his writings cited above do not display a deep understanding of the past, or of the human condition. Today, however, we are in a position to conclude, based on meticulous research, that history and language are interrelated, yet they are not one and the same.

There are events, conflicts and reconciliations that occur at a prelinguistic level and are communicated through signs. They also form a type of language. 'The more highly aggregated the units of action,' argues Reinhart Koselleck, 'the more important the conditions of linguistic communication become.'[29] It has been noted that by focusing on language one does not have to reduce the whole of history to a discussion of linguistics, but rather that language reflects the changes in social conditions over the course of history. This is why a detailed understanding of history is essential in this debate.[30] German academics at the end of the eighteenth and the beginning of the nineteenth century adopted a sentimental discourse that did not always reflect reality. Herder was one such ideologue – writing in an era that was moving towards modernity – whose theoretical speculations were not always in tune with lived experiences.

Furthermore, the social and political sciences were not sufficiently advanced or rigorous at this stage. Despite this, Immanuel Kant's objections to Herderianism cannot be attributed solely to the difference of opinion between the Romantics and the Enlightenment thinkers. After all, Herder himself was a product of the Enlightenment who had reaped the rewards of the *Aufklärung*'s literary, philosophical and historiographical creativity. Many of his ideas were inspired by the work of his contemporaries. While he greatly influenced the intelligentsia of Central, Eastern and Southeastern Europe – a feat not always recognised – Herder shaped the first theory of national identity not only in those regions, but especially in the German-speaking world. The idea of ethnoculturalism and the nation state being rooted in the spirit of a single ethnic group (*Volk*) is still very much alive today, notably in the political discourse of the former Communist states. The survival of this doctrine, which often amazes those who are not versed in the history of political ideas, cannot be explained simply in terms of the impulses of Herderianism or its Romantic followers. It is also rooted in the specific political conditions of that region and the conflicts it has experienced over the course of history.

III

THE NATION: THE MEANINGS OF A HISTORICAL-POLITICAL CONCEPT

1. WHAT IS A NATION?

In 1882, Ernest Renan delivered a lecture at the Sorbonne entitled *Qu'est-ce qu'une Nation?* (*What is a Nation?*), with the intention of exploring the concept from different perspectives. The result was one of the most influential texts about the history of French national identity,[1] one that is also a useful reference point for the interpretation of the ideology of the nation across all European culture. Considering it in hindsight after the experience of twentieth-century totalitarian regimes, *Qu'est-ce qu'une Nation?* seems prophetic, illustrating how 'fatal misunderstandings' of certain concepts can lead to great tragedies. The text also offers an insight into the political culture of Central, Eastern and Southeastern Europe, as it suggests these regions embraced a version of the historical concept of nation quite unlike the meaning it had acquired in France, England and the Netherlands. Renan's lecture highlights the conflicting doctrines of the past as well as the present, especially regarding cultures that have interpreted nation in a purely ethnographic sense. Written in the context of the Franco-Prussian War of 1870, *Qu'est-ce qu'une Nation?* was preceded by *La Guerre entre la France et l'Allemagne* (*The War Between France and Germany*).[2]

My aim here is to analyse Renan's message with regard to the formation of a united Europe as well as the integration of former Communist countries in the European federation. What was the main point of Renan's analysis? That the nation is 'an idea that seems clear and straightforward, but which, if misinterpreted, could prove dangerous'. Human experience has varied greatly over the course of history, and to ignore this would lead to serious misunderstandings of the past and the present. For example, Athens and Sparta were organised differently than autonomous states such as France or England; densely populated regions such as China, Egypt or ancient Babylon were unlike the Carolingian Empire, which was composed of different nations; communities without a nation – for example, the Jews in late antiquity and the Middle Ages – defined their identity through religion, setting them apart from communities that belonged to confederations such as Switzerland.

Renan distinguishes between nations with different socio-political structures, suggesting that it is impossible to adopt an umbrella term that would include all kinds of identities, as the historical context, as well as the religion, language and race of different communities, gives them their own specific characteristics:

> Classical antiquity featured republics, municipal royalty, confederations, local republics, empires; it did not have nations in the way we might understand the term... Athens, Sparta, Sidon and Tyre were centres of patriotism, but they were relatively small kingdoms. Before their absorption into the Roman Empire, Gaul, Spain and Italy were ensembles of communities often linked together, but without central institutions or dynasties. The Assyrian Empire, the Persian Empire and Alexander's empire were not homelands. There have never been Assyrian patriots; the Persian Empire was a vast feudal system. No nation traces its origins back to Alexander's colossal adventures, despite their significant impact on the general history of civilisation. The Roman Empire was closer than any of these to being a homeland... It

was associated with peace and civilisation, synonymous with order. During the last stages of the empire, a true feeling of 'Roman peace' that replaced chaotic barbarism was experienced by elevated souls such as enlightened priests and scholars. But an empire twelve times larger than present-day France cannot be described as a state in the modern sense.[3]

Ernest Renan possessed a profound understanding of classical civilisation, along with Jewish and Christian history, which allowed him to form his own theories regarding the past. He was particularly interested in social and political structures, but was also fascinated by great personalities and ground-breaking ideas, although he never favoured a metaphysical interpretation of history. The most important aspect of Renan's *Qu'est-ce qu'une Nation?* is its insistence that the past must be reinterpreted. Also noting the way in which the interpretation of facts changes from one era to another, he focused on the often conflicting connotations of the idea of nation. In his view, the empire built by Alexander the Great could not be described as a homeland, and therefore the concept of nation could not be applied to it; he pointed out the differences between the Roman civilisation and the French state, as well as ancient kingdoms and modern nations. Within the same text, he rejected the connection between the Merovingian era and the French Revolution of 1789.[4] Moreover, he aptly described the nation as 'a daily plebiscite, in the same way that the existence of the individual depends on the permanent concrete evidence put in the service of life'. On the other hand, echoing Michelet and Quinet, Renan argued that 'our predecessors determine who we are'.

The two different perspectives on the idea of the nation illustrate the opposition between past and present, history and law (or sociology), origins and contract, left and right.[5] Renan traces the problem of differentialism on the basis of nationality to the expansionism of early medieval administrations. For example, the invasion of the Germanic peoples stimulated differentiation as it contributed to the emergence of the military aristocracy, the establishment of dynasties, the diversification of racial groups and the fragmentation of the territories of the old Western Roman Empire. Communities were no longer divided from each other on the basis of religious differences, as both the victor and the conquered considered themselves to be Christians. The fact that the Germanic populations adapted to their new conditions and began to assimilate is reflected in the linguistic amalgamations that occurred as a result of them living side by side with the inhabitants of the conquered regions. Despite the extreme violence that characterised the first period of the conquests, a Frankish state emerged. When the reign of Hugh Capet came to an end, the state became an administrative body seemingly untroubled by racial differences, as there are none mentioned by French authors. Although many have commented on the distinctions between the nobility and the peasantry, relationships between ethnic groups did not appear to have been a pertinent subject.

Within the French state, distinctions between social groups were tolerated, as they had been passed down through generations. According to Renan, no French citizen would be aware whether he descended from the Burgundians or the Visigoths. It would be hard to find ten families in France that could trace their origins, something which makes the study of genealogy almost impossible.[6] In Turkey, on the other hand, the situation is completely different as the deliberate segregation of groups according to religion – for political reasons – had serious consequences. Renan cites as examples Thessaloniki and Smyrna, cities where five or six communities lived alongside each other, united by their shared memories but by little else. The chief characteristic of a nation is that it is a community of people bonded together by the many things they have in common:

> The birth of the modern nation resulted from a convergence of different factors. Occasionally, some degree of unification was achieved by a particular dynasty, as we have seen in the case of France; alternatively, the provinces created an alliance of their own accord, such as in Holland, Switzerland and Belgium; other times, a populist spirit was ignited in reaction to the excesses of the feudal system, as was the case in Italy and Germany. *In all of these cases, there was a strong sense of the people wanting to define themselves as a unit.* The biggest surprises of all have been the unification of Italy through defeats and the disappearance of Turkey as a result of victories. This is because Italy is a nation and Turkey is not.[7]

Certain ideas emerge from these historical evaluations. First of all, it is essential to remember that modernisation in Western Europe did not occur in a linear fashion and that various medieval traditions played different roles in the emancipation of certain social groups and the formation of nations. Second, it must be noted that the growth of literacy – albeit slow until the middle of the nineteenth century – had a major impact on the development of the modern state. As the historian Eric Hobsbawm has observed, one of the consequences of this spread of literacy was that schools and universities became the great promoters of nationalism.[8] In addition to Renan's observations, it is worth noting that the regions and peoples annexed by the Ottoman and Hapsburg empires had completely different experiences from those in Western Europe, and that their awakening to the bonds of language and tradition that united them came only between 1800 and 1848. Turkey was indeed an empire and not a nation, although it managed to claim this status during the twentieth century.

Differentialism practised on the basis of religion was not as harmful as the kind that occurred in Prussia, which was primarily ethnocultural. The Ottoman Empire, on the other hand, was remarkably tolerant of religious diversity in the Balkans, even though it did not encourage the formation of ethnocultures or identification with traditions. Constantinople was concerned with protecting the structure of its empire and therefore needed to subdue regional political aspirations. Furthermore, just like the Hapsburg and Tsarist empires, it did not see the regions it controlled as nations. Its identity was based on its power, its territories and the subordination of the people living there. In some cases, such as the Hapsburg Empire, it was possible to appease these populations by giving them the status of equal citizens of the empire. Such measures ensured the relatively peaceful coexistence of people who did not share a language or a culture.

How are national laws conceived? How do we determine whether an individual or a group is a part of a nation? What are the characteristics that define a nation? These were the pressing questions that emerged in the nineteenth century and were still being discussed a century later. For many intellectuals, there was only one answer: race. Unlike other, more fanciful theories, Renan's arguments are logical and critically sound. He was particularly concerned with interrogating the concept of ethnicity, which at the time was almost exclusively equated with race. In the second part of his famous 1882 lecture, which did not take into account how the ideology of *Völkischekultur* was interpreted in Central and Southeastern Europe, he asserted that the concept of nation was unrelated to ethnography. He was alarmed that German intellectuals and politicians saw racial purity and national identity as interlinked.

There was intense interest in the origins of humanity during this era, and many searched for the roots of the modern world in its early beginnings, attempting to discover archetypes and construct a linear narrative of history that would support their belief systems. This focus on national origins was combined with Darwinism, applying its theories about the evolution of plants and animals to the development of humankind.

In Prussia there was a fascination with purity of bloodline and the idea that cultural superiority derived from primitive origins. It manifested itself in an insistence on segregation, the conservation of different ethnic traditions and a focus on maintaining 'racial purity' through opposition to any attempt to pollute the bloodline. Renan foresaw the way this ideology could lead to the emergence of totalitarian regimes:

> Germanism exerts a greater power over the provinces than the rights of their own inhabitants. In this way, a primordial right was created that is analogous to the divine right of kings. The concept of the nation was substituted by ethnography. This is a grave mistake, because if this principle gains dominance, the European civilisation will be lost. While the concept of the nation is a just and legitimate one, the primordial right of the races is a narrow ideology which could impede real progress.[9]

The historian draws a comparison between this phenomenon and the French and English political traditions of the eighteenth century. The connotations of nation in the context of the French Revolution were very different from those it had acquired in Germany. It was not the first time that Renan noted the remnants of feudalism in the political culture of Germany. The fact that Germanism could override the rights of the individual – or that such an abstract idea could become law and gain more importance than the aspirations of particular communities – exposed the flaws in political thinking under Bismarck's reign.

Kulturnation emerged as the opposite concept to that of nation as understood by Western European cultures. The promotion of stereotypes could be observed in various academic disciplines, in literature and through the press. The theme of racial purity became so popular with the elite during the 1860s and 1870s that any rational attempt to challenge it was quickly suppressed as it was sustained by political structures. In the works of some writers, racism was transformed into 'the chief principle of German education' or the so-called 'stronghold of German education'.[10] Like the concept of ethnicity, the idea of race has no historical basis once we start to analyse the composition of each nation. Europe has been inhabited for a very long time. It is difficult to trace the roots, language and ethnic origins of every group of people. Geographical location provides a reference point for the beginnings of a civilisation, but it is not enough to support a theory of national unity based on race.

Ethnography is irrelevant to national identity as it is to any political theme relating to modern and contemporary history. Although in Ancient Greece or among the tribes of the Near East the question of race might have had some significance, the same is not true of the Roman Empire. Renan argues that 'the tribe and the ancient city were simply extensions of the family. In Sparta and Athens all the citizens were in some way related.' Undoubtedly, human experience was different in the ancient world. The Roman Empire, however, represented 'the key point of departure from the idea of race'. Its vast size and population with numerous towns and provinces, as well as its colonialist expansion that entailed the mobilisation of its army and administration, meant that the isolation of any group of people was impossible. In such circumstances, the preservation of racial purity was untenable.

Why should the Germanic peoples be an exception to this rule, therefore, considering that medieval Europe was founded on the cosmopolitan civilisations of the Roman and Carolingian empires? Is it possible that this community retained its racial purity over the centuries? 'Nonsense!... France is Celtic, Iberian and Germanic.

Germany is Germanic, Celtic and Slavic... The entire South was Gallic. The entire East, starting from Elba, was Slavic.'[11] Renan believed that these 'arguments about race would never be resolved because philological historians and physiological anthropologists have completely different interpretations of the word. The anthropologists understand race in the same way that it is applied to zoology: it refers to literal genetic inheritance. *However, the study of languages or history cannot produce such clear, straightforward distinctions.*'[12]

His observations seem all the more significant considering the way racial theories became increasingly popular with the elite and the masses during this period. Like Renan, I also see the history of Europe as marked by common social and political interests, a long struggle for identity and for national structures embedded in religious and cultural traditions. It is an archive of diverse human testimonies, conflicts and tragedies. In a chapter dedicated to the problems and vicissitudes of European unity, Isaiah Berlin emphasised the fact that there are many important similarities between the continent's individuals, cultures and nations. In comparison, differences are relatively few and fairly unimportant.[13] His answer to those who fanatically disseminate the propaganda that nation is related to blood ties is that one human characteristic is much more important than language, religion, skin colour, social background or geographical location – rationality. This characteristic enables us to grasp the ultimate truth of life, both on a theoretical and a practical level.

Renan invoked a number of rational arguments, drawing from the field of contemporary social sciences, to reject the historical, philological and philosophical speculations of German Romanticism:

That which from a philological and historical point of view is described as the Germanic race is indeed a distinct human community. But can it be considered a family in the anthropological sense? Certainly not. Historically, the emergence of German identity dates back to the centuries before Jesus Christ. However, it seems that the Germans were not concentrated in one particular territory. They had merged with the Slavs within the great amorphous mass of the Scythians and did not have any distinct identity. An Englishman truly is a prototype for the whole of humanity. This prototype, which we mistakenly call the Anglo-Saxon race, is neither the Breton of Caesar's time, nor the Anglo-Saxon Hengist, nor the Danish Knut, nor the Norman William the Conqueror: it is the sum of all this. The instinctive conscience that presided over the construction of the European map did not take race into account at all, and the first nations of Europe were the result of a mixture of blood. Human history differs significantly from zoology.[14]

Where did the idea originate that a community was defined by its racial purity? Why did this misconception capture the imagination of so many Enlightenment scholars, who essentially belonged to the same civilisation? Who were the chief promoters of *Volksgeist* (the congenital spirit of the people, the spirit of the race) and why did they propagate these confused doctrines? Hamann, Fichte, Herder and the whole of the German literary movement known as *Sturm und Drang* placed themselves in extreme opposition to the values of the Enlightenment. According to these writers, a nation had to be formed through the invention of an ideal, united people. And how could this be achieved? Through poetry. Herder believed that only the poet could win hearts and lead them in the right direction. He was a god on Earth. From here to the position assumed by the visionaries who conceived the philosophy of *das Volk* there was only one small step. The idea of consanguinity permeates the entire German Romantic discourse on the subject of the nation and the nation state.

In this way, the concept that the ideal state is formed of a single people, with their own specific characteristics, their own particular songs, language and spirit, took root in German culture. The purism of *das Volk* was often associated with linguistic purism, but there were also differences between them. In *The Crooked Timber of Humanity*, Isaiah Berlin claims that this was the beginning of nationalism and even populism, of the cult of heroes and leaders, as well as brutal irrationalism.[15]

Renan noticed the way the ideas of the Romantics had evolved over time and been used to construct arguments regarding race, as well as the fact that language had acquired a political dimension. It was these erroneous theories that prompted his historical analysis of language. He argued that all these concepts had little to do with bloodlines, despite claims to the contrary: 'In any case, language is no barrier to human freedom when it comes to choosing a family.'[16] Any speculation concerning language or race is fraught with danger. Renan believed that the insistence on the value of a national language could impede the appreciation of a universal culture. He argued that before humans acquired any language or specific characteristics, they were, above all, rational creatures. This, he claimed, was the fundamental principle that should never be overlooked.[17] Cultural propaganda – aided by historiography and literature – had established an ideology based on conflict, which prompted Renan to construct a coherent and logical narrative of history.

Is there anything we might question about his theories? Occasionally he emphasises the ancient and medieval origins of the modern nation. It seems reasonable to argue that the modern era owes a debt to the past, particularly if we see it as the result of the breakdown of the feudal system. However, there are many differences between the medieval royal courts and the economic, political and cultural specificities of modern capitalist states. Only vague similarities can be established between the religious feudal hierarchy and modern societies. The state was led by the nobility, namely a king with prerogatives derived from historical law and an elite formed exclusively by heredity, which provoked the revolt of the new nobility in England, the third state in France and the commercial bourgeoisie in the Netherlands. The result was rebellion against the system. The political strategies, organisational and administrative typology, legislation and institutions, social structures and hierarchies, as well as the cultural aspirations of the modern age, suggest that it is very different from the feudal world.

Renan focused excessively on the way these arguments were formulated in the past, despite the fact that the concept of nation was already being reinvented by the modern era. This problem exists even today, as historians continue to evoke previous interpretations of the nation state. For example, Fernand Braudel's theory of 'longue durée' (long duration) – based on his analysis of the economic developments that took place during the transition from the medieval to the modern period – is flawed when it attempts to describe social institutions and political thought, as it claims that our modern society is merely an extension of previous ones. In L'Identité de la France (The Identity of

France), Braudel claims that the French nation has remained unchanged since the Middle Ages. Even though his analysis extends only to the beginning of the nineteenth century, he implies that the concept of nation has not changed in the subsequent two hundred years.[18]

It is inevitable that as old principles have merged with new there is a sense of continuity between the past and the present. It is important to realise, however, that this focus on continuity can blind us to the specificity of the present. In particular, some regions have developed more slowly due to the conservatism of previous political leaders. For example, in Ukraine, the persistence of feudalism and its associated political structures in the eighteenth century greatly delayed modernisation. The aristocracy was so intent on protecting its privileges that it placed obstacles in the way of progress. Eventually, the new ideas managed to permeate its society as a result of commerce, military conflicts and migration (particularly from Russia), but they also resulted in interethnic tensions.[19] This example presents a different type of continuity from that suggested by Michelet or Braudel. When comparing Renan's reflections with Braudel's theory of '*longue durée*', the former seems to capture more accurately the different European identities currently concerned with discovering what unites them rather than divides them. *Qu'est-ce qu'une Nation?* offers a more cohesive perspective on culture than the ideas of Braudel and others who share his approach. Renan's analysis often evades the subject of historical continuity, as his main objective was to expose the flawed political arguments of the second half of the nineteenth century. His perspective on the modern concept of nation seems particularly significant when considering how the errors made in 'the century of the nation' were subsequently repeated. *Qu'est-ce qu'une Nation?* references the past but does not lose sight of the modern context and political significance of nation. The analysis of how this concept developed over previous centuries is presented as significant only inasmuch as it opens up new ways of interpreting the present.

History gives a sense of coherence to events, categories and concepts. Renan's writings highlighted the confused dogmas of the past and the inadequate response of certain intellectuals and politicians to contemporary issues. *Qu'est-ce qu'une Nation?* is a seminal text in the field of historiography and offers an important evaluation of modern political theories. Renan was one of only a handful of thinkers who foresaw that the juxtaposition of French and German perspectives could lead to a global conflict. His emphasis on the differences between their concepts of nation illuminates the significance of context when it comes to formulating this ideal. In the light of past and present European developments, Renan's work allows us to examine the relationship between the specific and the general, between the national and the transnational. Many of these conflicts remained unresolved and therefore destabilised the European social order.

As mentioned, the modern concept of nation entails a unified consciousness, the sense that the feelings and actions of every member of society are orientated towards the same purpose. This concept took on a revolutionary identity as soon as it positioned itself in opposition to feudal privilege and sought its annihilation. In Western Europe, a new world order was created when the power invested in the divine sovereignty of the monarchy was transferred to the parliament or national assembly. However, 'the spirit of the people' did not generate a political transformation. Instead, it remained only a confused concept that enabled the elites of the nineteenth and twentieth centuries to protect their privilege by channelling the masses' desire to throw off their medieval servitude and take a new direction, thereby giving them the illusion of emancipation. As a result, the feudal nobility in certain parts of Europe was slow to adapt to a new mode of thinking. By placing ethnoculture at the root of the ethnonation, there was an emphasis on the bonds between people created over time. Clearly, feudal power relationships persisted in the rural areas, where modernisation was limited and benefited only certain socio-economic groups – where the middle classes did not exist and illiteracy was the norm.

The propagation of flawed ideas about genealogy within historical narratives – a tendency rightly criticised by Renan – did not merely generate a distorted cultural perspective, but also created an ideology with serious consequences. These ideas were endowed with a great deal of authority and exploited to justify a social order based on spurious theories about origins. Such trends can be observed in the history of the modernisation of Prussia and later in Germany, Greece, the Austro-Hungarian Empire, Serbia, Romania and Bulgaria. This is the reason why any serious survey of intellectual history must focus on the use of language in any given period. According to medieval constitutional historian Otto Brunner, we need to grasp the language used to define certain concepts in a particular era before we can translate it into our own words.[20]

2. THE CONCEPT OF NATION IN CONTEMPORARY EUROPE

It is essential to comprehend the problem of national identity as it plays a vital role in shaping a society's perception of its environment.[21] What are the current connotations of the concept of nation and how do they differ from those outlined in Renan's famous 1882 public lecture? Any honest communication on this topic is often impeded by self-regard, hence it is important to reopen this discussion. While a century ago there was a conflict between the French and German interpretations of national identity, today the question of differentialism is topical in Europe's central regions. To what extent are the Centre, East and Southeast of the continent attempting to redefine their cultural and political character? Can these states adopt the same interpretation of national identity as those of Western Europe? Will they align themselves with a wider European culture rather than champion national differences?

The supranational unity of the continent – supported by federal administration – will need to take into account the particularist-ethnographic tendencies of the former Communist countries that have been key to their exploration of their own past, but which may become problematic as they attempt to adapt to the dynamics of the Western world. This process necessitates an understanding of the subtleties of Western political thought and accepting that those European entities that were excluded from the exchange of cultural values and free movement of ideas after the Second World War now seek to redefine their identities.

First, it is important to remember that the nation state continues to play a role in the collective memory of all Europeans. Second, it should be noted that the majority of the inhabitants of the old continent still place a greater value on their national, rather than European, identity. Undoubtedly, a concept may have different connotations in various languages. However, the connotations of the concept of nation depend on many factors: cultural traditions, administrative-institutional structures, favourable economic conditions for the diversification of professions and intellectual pursuits, religious orientation, literary-philosophical activities, and so on. All of these can have a significant effect on the interpretation of this particular ideology. For now, let us note that the East and the West approach the concept of national identity in different ways. Third, despite several parallels, the political cultures of Western Europe also vary in their interpretation of the concept in question. A number of attributes are listed in independent ontological studies. Anthony Smith identifies the following: a common history and a common territory, a common culture, a certain level of economic development and integration, and a coherent constitution and political-administrative system.

These attributes do not apply to every nation. To promote a set of common values ensuring a harmonious European civilisation, national characteristics must be attenuated. The aspirations of contemporary Europe are not identical to those of nineteenth-century Europe. Therefore, the national project cannot be viewed in the same way as it was during the capitalist revolution. Furthermore, the idea of the nation was re-evaluated following the demise of the regimes of Hitler and Stalin. In *La Guerre entre la France et l'Allemagne*, Renan observes that 'We will see the end of war when the principle of nationality will be replaced by a superior principle: that of the European federation, superior to all nationalities'.[22] Renan's comment accurately describes the political orientation of most Western European states today. Reflecting on the conflicts across Europe during the past century, it is plausible to see that a particular version of nation played an important role in creating the divisions to which Renan alludes. By emphasising the importance of geography, ethnicity and religion in shaping national identity, some states lost sight of the principles that could unite them and support their collective endeavours.

It should also be added that the Western European idea of the nation has undergone a certain transformation during the post-war period. For example, laws protecting cultural and religious minorities have been put in place to combat intolerance of otherness;

ethnocultural identity (in the case of Germany)[23] has superseded social and civic identity; instead of territorial disputes, we now have open borders; the racist and anti-Semitic rhetoric used in speeches about nation at the beginning of the century has been replaced by a discourse inherited from the Enlightenment that privileges racial tolerance, distinct cultures and intellectual progress.

The Romantic fantasy that instigated interstate and international conflicts has ceased to engage the world of academia and education. Rational analytical thinking has replaced the sentimentalist ideological excesses that shaped European history until the end of the Second World War. Within the humanities, the study of history has assumed the role of providing a critique of past facts and events and the lessons these might teach us about the human condition, rather than promoting legends. The myth of the national genius has fallen from favour, and a new ideal of the educated man, whose knowledge must respond to social, political and economic challenges, has taken its place. After a century-long period of global influence, Herderian and Fichtean spiritual nationalism no longer defines collective identity in Western Europe. Although this is rarely considered by Eastern European historians, Western historiography has abandoned any methodological and conceptual association between human history and the natural sciences.[24]

Many variations in the way the concept of nation is explored exist today in academic discourse and political thought. Often there is a close relationship between the nation, the citizen and democracy, and these terms are greatly interrelated. However, in many cultures these terms have acquired different (and sometimes contradictory) meanings, illustrating why decoding the significance of national identity is sometimes problematic.

We should consider the localised Irish, Basque and Corsican conflicts, as well as the struggles for power between larger European states. Local discord reflects the intense feeling of belonging to a community, which is exacerbated by the survival of regional traditions coupled with a dissatisfaction with the management of public affairs or a centralisation of power that has created imbalances in economic and social life. Such conflicts have an ethnic dimension in common, pointing back to the previously discussed ideology of nation. Nevertheless, apart from these exceptions, in the contemporary world nation is generally understood as a political structure. For this type of nation, the focus is no longer on territorial disputes, but on creating effective institutions, the common administration of goods, the exploitation of resources and the promotion of strategic interests through foreign policy.

Some authors maintain that national identity is the sum of our history, beliefs and outlooks, which accumulate over time to create the collective memory of a society. Ilya Prizel believes that 'national identity serves not only as the first link between the individual and society, but also as the link between the individual and the world'.[25] By the same token, all countries frequently use their national identity to justify their foreign policy. Some intellectuals argue that the countries that use their foreign policy to strengthen their identities are those where the political elite feels most vulnerable and whose national identity is based on the cultural heritage of the Romantic era rather than functional institutions.

The term nation not only applies to the foreign policy of a state. First of all, it presupposes a social contract based on the desire of individuals to unite and create a cohesive community that enables their institutions to function. Furthermore, a European nation's foreign policy becomes inextricably linked to continental foreign policy. The European Union aims to formulate policies that create a coherent relationship between the continent and America, Asia and the Arab world. Consequently, national differentialism in foreign policy will give way to transnational or supranational political strategy.

In countries where foreign policy favours the ruling elite, legal institutions play a marginal role in the nation-building process. This tendency is especially true in states where Romantic nationalism prevails. In these countries, foreign policy assumes disproportionate influence and the elite uses the ideology of national prestige, symbols and rights to their advantage. This can have a significant impact on the dynamics of national identity. The former Communist states are far more prone to this than Western European countries. Certain nations could provide a model for creating the ideal European identity. In many ways, contemporary Europe resembles nineteenth-century Switzerland, where the civic republican myth was created by a federal state built on universal suffrage. This was imposed by a liberal elite that promoted an idea of national identity that embraced all the linguistic groups of the cantons. In Europe, on the other hand, political structures created by the elite still feature institutions that do not fully integrate all of its communities.

Europe needs a civic myth, one that can help shape its federal identity. According to Hanspeter Kriesi, the first step in creating the European nation is the existence of a democratic policy in all states that prepares them to become members of this federation. This does not merely entail the democratisation of political institutions. The European nation can be viable only if it promotes the civic myth of European unity which will give rise to 'constitutional patriotism'. This unity promises the development of an identity based on common values, symbols and a shared, continental memory.[26] The civic spirit has much more to offer to the European nations than individual national identities built on ethnic bonds.[27] Europeans are generally closely connected to multiple levels of government and, with the exceptions of Great Britain and Sweden, the majority of countries seem very attached to the European identity. Switzerland's experience provides a key as to how the myth of a unified Europe might be formed. What might this entail? Kriesi argues that many different nations could benefit from transforming old traditions into new ones. The history of Europe itself provides sufficient material which could be used to build a common European tradition.

3. WHY DOES THE CONCEPT OF NATION NEED TO BE REDEFINED IN RELATION TO CENTRAL AND SOUTHEASTERN EUROPE?

The previous chapters of this book emphasise that concepts need to adapt to different cultural and historical contexts. Such views shape daily life as well as political theories. As far as the concept of nation is concerned, it has acquired various connotations over time, ranging from the abstract and metaphysical to the rational and practical. The question of national identity has been discussed in numerous historical and sociological works. Unfortunately, it is not always analysed rationally, as many thinkers still dwell on speculations rooted in the Romantic ideology of the nation; a certain dogmatic ignorance still perpetuates an image of the past and ideology of the nation that echo the myths created at the beginning of the modern era. These historical, sociological and philosophical studies, although well researched and informed by the latest theories, tend to focus on a different concept of nation from the one now widely accepted in the West. The influence of German culture on the countries of Central and Southeastern Europe resulted in their adoption of the organic idea of the nation.

The fact that *Volksgeist* is still at the core of the political cultures of these regions is due to the fact that their Communist heritage has problematised their identity, an idea not always understood by their Western European neighbours. The concept of nation was redefined in the political sphere of these countries either as a result of the disinformation practised within them or the combination of Stalinist ideology with a Fascist brand of ethnonationalism. The political culture of Central and Southeastern Europe did not allow for a more modern social, judicial and historical definition of the concept to emerge. Commenting on the phenomenon of nationalism, G. M. Tamás makes the following interesting observation:

> The most extreme form of ethnocultural nationalism has become very influential, yet it cannot offer answers to political problems. Instead, it is a reaffirmation of identity. In the nineteenth century, nationalism made the state stronger; twentieth-century nationalism disregards all institutions; it is anarchic, defying the state and its structures.[28]

We will consider this statement in more detail, focusing particularly on its contradictions. First of all, nineteenth-century nationalism created territorial disputes, insisting on the superior rights of the indigenous population and consolidating the status of those who inherited power from the past medieval administration. A doctrine that insists on the importance of geography above all else can only be described as arbitrary. Can it really be true that a nation is defined by the outline of a map? Ernest Renan correctly predicted that if such ideas permeated political thought, they would lead to violence.[29] Ethnonationalism did not strengthen the state, as G. M. Tamás claims, particularly as Eastern European states emerged much later than those of Western Europe.

Historian Jules Michelet's works *Histoire de France* (1833) and *Le Peuple* (1846) mobilised the myth of brotherhood and solidarity inherent in the French Revolutionaries' key concept of *peuple*. *Below*, 1794 allegorical engraving advocating Revolutionary France's cult of the supreme being. Voltaire (standing beside a bust of the tyrannicide Brutus) and Rousseau direct us towards the 'sovereign people' at the centre of the image.

Johann Gottfried Herder, whose conception of *Volk* and the *Kulturnation* paved the way to national and ethnic consciousness in nineteenth-century Germany. *Below*, Friedrich Gunkel's monumental painting *Die Hermannsschlacht* (1862–4) epitomises Germany's construction of the archetypal 'ethnic being', in this case the chieftain Arminius ('Hermann') who defeated the Romans in the Teutoburg Forest in AD 9.

Frédéric Sorrieu and Marie-Cécile Goldsmid's 1848 lithograph celebrates Europe's 'year of revolutions', though due to different rates of development and notions of nationhood, the impact of these social movements varied greatly from country to country. *Below*, an 1848 depiction of Romanian revolutionaries: for a brief period that year, intellectuals from Wallachia were concerned with creating a national identity that would benefit the country's entire population.

Ernest Renan, whose 1882 lecture *Qu'est-ce qu'une Nation?* identified the differences between the French and German conceptions of nationhood and foresaw the ways in which the Prussian preoccupation with bloodline would lead to totalitarianism and war. *Below*, Anton von Werner's painting from three years later (he had produced earlier versions in 1877 and 1882, now lost) celebrates Wilhelm I's investiture as the first German Emperor in the Palace of Versailles in 1871, following France's defeat in the Franco-Prussian War – the original context of Renan's research.

Mosque and marketplace in Sarajevo, Austria-Hungary, c.1910. *Below*, the Moda cricket team from Istanbul, photographed for the 1896 season. Both the Hapsburg and Ottoman empires exercised multiculturalism and plurilingualism in their rule of Central and Southeastern Europe, qualities that led to their destabilisation and eventual demise as nationalism enforced an image of cultural unity.

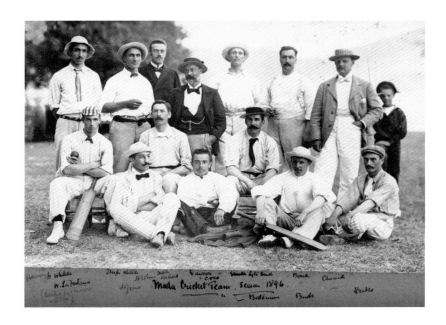

The declaration of Transylvania's union with Romania, at the National Assembly in Alba Iulia, 1 December 1918. The opportunity to re-evaluate history and bring the region's Romanian, German and Hungarian communities together was squandered in favour of centrist conservative policies from Bucharest. *Below*, the resulting ethno-nationalism gave rise to Romania's Fascist Iron Guard, here being inspected by its leader Corneliu Codreanu in 1934.

Nicolae Ceaușescu's 'folkloric myth' on the world stage, during US President Gerald Ford's visit to Bucharest in 1975. *Below*, the overthrow of the nationalist Communist regime in 1989 began in Timișoara in the Banat region, whose society (like those of Brașov and Sibiu) embraced its diverse cultural heritage and had long looked to the West for inspiration.

'Kin' against integration: members of the Hungarian far-right Jobbik party flood Warsaw city centre on Polish Independence Day, 11 November 2015, to protest against immigration in the European Union. *Below*, the enduring power of the myth of *peuple*: Pascal Boyart's Paris mural dedicated to the *gilets jaunes* protests of the end of 2018 is based on Delacroix's *La Liberté guidant le peuple*, itself a redeployment of symbols from 1789 in the context of the July Revolution of 1830.

Nationalism created an image of cultural unity that would be exploited by politicians to create the nation state. This new consciousness destabilised the Ottoman and Hapsburg empires and led to their eventual downfall. However, ethnocultural nationalism appeared only in certain European regions. Apart from Switzerland and a few other small Western European countries, it was characteristic of Central and Southeastern Europe. It was inherited from German culture and promoted by intellectuals with the intention of developing a unified consciousness in their own lands. However, before the modern era, the populations of the Balkan Peninsula saw their Orthodox religion, rather than ethnicity, as the foundation of their identity.

On the other hand, Tamás is correct to assert that twentieth-century ethnonationalism disregarded state institutions. However, I would add that it did not limit itself to reaffirming identity, but that, as early as its revolutionary beginnings, it intended to create artificial divisions between groups of people by overemphasising the role of language and traditions, therefore preparing the ground for violent conflict. In Yugoslavia, ethnonationalism was not merely a nostalgic expression of identity, but the ideological engine of its civil wars. In relation to this example, I am inclined to agree with Danilo Kiš's definition of nationalism – primarily applied to its Eastern and Southeastern European interpretation – as first and foremost the symptom of a collective and individual paranoia that corrodes individual conscience.

To understand the significance of the ethnonation in the context of the political culture of the former Communist states of Central and Southeastern Europe, we need a rational re-evaluation of the history of the past two centuries. The concept of nation needs to be redefined through the lens of *societas civilis* (civil society).

History has witnessed the formation of both totalitarian ideologies and democratic structures, so we must study it to understand how national consciousness is created. The historian Jenő Szűcs and the political analyst István Bibó have considered the formation of political structures in Central Europe and beyond. Through historical enquiry, we can compare the superior rationality of European thinkers during the Enlightenment period with the Romantic phantasmagoria that followed. In this light, it seems vital to reclaim the idea of nation as a civic institution rather than becoming mired in disputes over territory and geography, pure origins or religious mysticism. It is precisely in the regions where these Enlightenment principles were not well known or failed to take root that they are needed most for their populations to become truly emancipated. This could provide a way to transcend provincialism and develop relationships between different regions of the continent. Western and Eastern states are united by a belief in the nation, but it is a concept that differs in its meaning from one area to another. However, they all value the balanced, rational approach to life promoted by eighteenth-century thinkers. This does not require the loss of distinct traditions, but it tempers cultural and political hubris. For the European project of integration to succeed, the language of these different regions needs to become harmonised.

What does this mean? It is important to insist on the close relationship between words and deeds. For example, the concepts of nation, state and federation have evolved significantly over time and in academic and political debates. Their meaning should not differ dramatically across various parts of the continent. The ideology of the ethnonation should not be used to forge national identity as long as it promotes discrimination between different groups based on linguistic heritage or encourages the dangerous powers of separatism.

We began with the idea that ethnicity is not synonymous with nation. There are many multi-ethnic states that can be described as nations, such as Belgium, the Netherlands and Switzerland, as previously discussed. These states have been structured in ways that have enabled social and national cohesion. Conversely, the doctrine of ethnoculture in Eastern Europe inhibits political dialogue in such a way that common interests and suprastate integration are compromised.

Policies created to address 'the question of minorities' play an important role in this discussion. Centuries ago, cities like Prague, Vienna, Budapest, Chernivtsi, Lviv, Bratislava and Timișoara were seen as the prototypes of pluralistic societies in Central Europe. These were the multicultural experiments of the modern era, where tribal segregation was kept at bay through social and political endeavours. They could serve as models for the creation of an environment – be it a city or a nation – where different religious and ethnic communities could coexist harmoniously, highlighting the difference between *demos* and *ethnos*. At this new junction in political life, the civic spirit can drive national identity in a different direction and transcend ethnic divisions.

The common goal of political liberalism can be achieved only through the promotion of tolerance. Currently, in Central and Southeastern Europe a superficial kind of civic education appears to be in fashion, which eschews social reality (in some countries more than others), promotes confused ideologies and lacks a clear purpose. The most important intercultural and transcultural perspectives are those which prepare future generations for a democratic way of life. So far, however, it is the monocultural discourse that dominates public dialogue and there is a clear contradiction between theory and practice. Personal political interests are prioritised rather than the rights of minorities.[30]

Undoubtedly, it is impossible to achieve unification between states without a common goal. The European Union requires not only an agreement on various legal rights, but the economic and social cohesion of communities that until now have defined themselves only in relation to their national identities. True unification can only be achieved by championing the common values shared by the member states and sacrificing the sovereignty that played such a central role in the idea of nation. While the formation of national identity initially required a consolidation of specific cultural values, these are now anachronistic as the nation states need to adapt to the standards of the European Union.

An ethnonation that continues to define itself as an ethnoculture is unable to adapt to a new political climate, as opposed to one that particularly treasures its individual identity. Certain sectors of these societies hide their political perspectives behind the notion that they are trying to preserve their ancient collective identity. Many political leaders exploit the fact that the rural population and those who have only recently settled in an urban environment have limited access to accurate information and therefore present the ideal audience for nationalist propaganda. Their cause is aided by the poor economic performance of post-Communist governments. In his book *Fantasies of Salvation*, Vladimir Tismăneanu accurately notes that the end of Communism resulted in a collective anxiety and feeling of disorientation that gave rise to a new ethnonationalist mythology. This ideology reflected an idealised past, suggesting that only by returning to these values could countries restore their hopes, pride and the dignity of the nation.[31]

The rise of ethnic nationalism created hostility towards the 'other', which also verged on an antipathy towards the West and threatened to marginalise these states. Western Europe did not exist as a political entity after the fall of Communism, something that created a sense of confusion for Central and Southeastern European states. They were expecting to find a fixed point of reference to redefine their own identities. Instead, they realised that the West was also in the process of reinventing itself ideologically; in other words, it was experiencing its own identity crisis. This led to a complex relationship between East and West.[32] Many academics, particularly from the former Communist countries, see this ethnonationalism – often standing in the way of reform and integration into the wider European political system – as a reaction against Soviet domination. Ilya Prizel and Maria Todorova, for instance, argue that this was the case in Poland, Romania and Bulgaria. As Soviet influence had dominated the period following the Second World War, many turned their attention back to theories developed during the interwar period. This is one of the chief reasons for the survival of the prejudices inherent in the Romantic concept of nation that prevailed at the time. Over the past decade, the cultural and political discourse of Central and Southeastern European states has been problematic and confused. One of the struggles has been the redefinition of the concept of nation, which reflects political perspectives and entails the re-evaluation of historical discourse and the discussion of ideas relating to European integration.

IV

KIN AND PEOPLE: THE CHARACTERISTICS OF ROMANIAN ETHNOCENTRISM

1. GEOGRAPHICAL VARIATIONS OF EUROPEAN CULTURE AND POLITICS

The decades following the Second World War have demonstrated Western Europe's desire to redefine some of the concepts on which its political identity was founded during the nineteenth and twentieth centuries, as evidenced in academic research and the political arena. There is a keen desire to promote pluralistic discourse and to embed this within laws, coupled with an acknowledgement that despite these efforts, the disquieting echoes of the old ideologies of national identities still persist. On the other hand, Eastern Europe is faced with an even more complex problem, as its slow recovery from the grip of two distinct totalitarian systems impedes its progress towards social and political democracy. In the countries of this region, nationalistic discourse has filled the vacuum left by the collapse of Communism. These states are just beginning their journey towards integration into a European system whose aims are still inadequately grasped by the general population.

If Western Europe maintains social harmony through its stable political structures, Eastern Europe seeks to win over the masses by promoting ethnocultural values that promise to unify them. While in the West there is a desire to examine the key terms that have been used to define national identity through history, paying attention to the way they have evolved through particular social and political climates, Eastern Europe feels an impulse to resurrect bygone values that appear to oppose Communist ideology. While Western Europe possesses an appetite for confronting the realities of the past, Eastern Europe prefers to turn a blind eye to the darkest moments of its history.

There is one exception within the European Union, however: Greece. The country stays close to its Balkan roots and, on the question of identity, its rhetoric oscillates between state bureaucracy and a discourse that privileges race and blood ties. The latter emerges from its cultural history, founded on eighteenth-century German ideologies and promoted through its educational system over the past two centuries. There is also a political dimension to the revival of Hellas as imagined by eighteenth-century German academics, as it seemed an auspicious foundation of modern, European, Greek identity.[1] Although the passage of time dulls human memory, there are certain patterns and structures that are inevitably absorbed within national consciousness through repetition and go on to deepen and enrich its culture.[2] According to Reinhart Koselleck, history is fragmented, making it impossible to trace the exact origins of a people. When discussing the institutions and cultural identity of Greece, we must consider the differences between its ancient incarnation and the neo-Hellenic world, in order to avoid making tenuous arguments. Unfortunately, today in Greece there is 'a centripetal cultural movement, and the historian only recognises a single point of departure, namely Athens in the fifth century BC'.[3]

This kind of cultural and historical reasoning is typical of Central and Eastern European states, for example, Romania. The cultural and political elite present their arguments as 'indisputable' facts. In a much-quoted article entitled 'The Balkan Socrates and the Socratic Caragiale', Alexandru Paleologu alleges that Greek philosophy, architecture and tragedy were 'indisputably the foundation of European civilisation', meaning that this civilisation has 'Balkan roots'. This becomes a leitmotif throughout the article, reflecting not only an ideological confusion but nostalgia for the dusty concepts of nineteenth-century literature and historiography:

> The fact that Socrates, Plato and Aristotle were Balkan is so often ignored seems strange to me. Some claim that Balkanism is a recent idea. That is not the case. If we see it as a concept tied to a particular geographical region and its population, then it must apply to the whole history of that place; on the other hand, if it is instead a localised, ephemeral phenomenon, then we cannot claim that it is inherent to any particular structure.

It is 'obvious', he concludes, 'that there is something eternal, quintessential, that has survived intact since antiquity'.[4] Such sweeping, metaphorical statements about different periods of time do not illuminate either the past or the present. Instead, they are evidence that intellectuals, non-academics and elected officials often rely on stereotypes.

There are marked differences between the rhetoric used in Eastern and Western Europe when discussing such topics, and in particular the question of political identity. Of course, no part of the continent is exempt from some kind of identity crisis at one point or another in history. The sources of these conflicts are often the same, and the elites of every country tend to gravitate towards similar ideals. However, when we look at each case in detail, we find significant differences between the ways such ideologies are interpreted, depending on their social context.

All too often, political commentators understate the differences that reflect the variety of cultural and political trends in different European states. Some compare the desire expressed by a proportion of the population in Northern Italy for regional or local autonomy to the divisions that led to the breakdown of Czechoslovakia or Yugoslavia, ignoring these countries' different social structures. Similarly, the same intellectuals see parallels between Spanish-Catalan bilingualism and the Transylvanian multiculturalism of contemporary Romania, as if there was an extraordinary equivalence between these two places on opposite sides of Europe.[5] The relationship between culture and political structure is complex and varies from one country to another.[6]

My research focuses on historical theories and their application to Eastern Europe, particularly Romania. In my opinion, although there is a convergence between the intellectual histories of different regions in Europe due to their common roots in the Enlightenment,[7] there are significant differences between the continent's East and West. In particular, I have in mind the Romanian terminology used to define collective identity. First of all, I shall discuss the term *neam* (kin) and its connotations in terms of national identity. One of the problems intellectuals face when attempting to create a common European discourse – for example, in relation to the European Constitution – is related to the conflicting ideologies that fuel political arguments in the Western and Eastern regions. I will explore how these ideologies come into being through language, which is used to define national identity and shaped by distinct cultural characteristics.

One problem is that the term nation (or people) had a specific resonance within Central and Eastern European political culture long before the existence of this Constitution. To be precise, the concept first and foremost defines a cultural and geographical cohesion that precedes any legal process. In the case of Eastern Europe, it is vital to consider the ethnonationalist values inherited from the nineteenth century, particularly Romanticism, which still compete with contemporary European values. This spectre of history in politics, particularly the revival and manipulation of cultural myths, is frequently incompatible with modern European values, as evidenced in the conflict in Yugoslavia. In that case, the Western powers that sought to resolve these tragic territorial conflicts clearly did not fully understand the ideology that informed them.

The differences between the two halves of the continent have become a point of interest for academics in the European Union. In an article published in *Frankfurter Rundschau*, Richard Wagner outlines the dilemma facing Eastern Europe today. Although Eastern Europeans

> do not trust the new West, led by Germany and France, they cannot conceive of a future outside the EU or NATO. Their desire to be part of the structure does not stem from an urge to modernise or regulate their own societies, but from a need to find some protection after being destabilised by the collapse of the Soviet bloc.

The author adds that Eastern Europeans are naturally more attracted to 'the individualist model of American society whose goal is personal fulfilment, rather than the West European ideology of social security and careful regulation. This is reflected in the weak, often anarchic, social structures that characterise Eastern Europe.'[8] Although I am not convinced that Eastern European states favour the individualist model, I agree with Wagner's idea that there is a significant difference between American society and that of post-Communist countries. This stark contrast is due to the fact that American society is founded on an idea of citizenship and a set of laws tailored to its own culture, while national identity in Eastern Europe is tied to the Romantic notion of *Kulturnation*, which still exerts greater influence than the state or the reforms required to assimilate it into a larger European structure.

Concepts generate modes of discourse, and these reflect the connections between the social and the political. History plays an important role in illuminating these connections. The social and political tendencies found in contemporary Eastern Europe began with the modern era, though clearly they often evolved in a different direction from their Western counterparts. For example, if we examine social behaviours in rural settings or in the peripheries of the larger cities, we see the influence of the family, the Church and the education system on their common values. In Serbia, Albania, Romania and Greece, national myths are still at the centre of political and cultural institutions. Philosophers such as Karl Popper have highlighted the impact of education and literacy on the emergence of the myth of the nation and the impact this has had on subsequent political discourse.

The identity of Central and Eastern Europe has been defined by its linguists, historians, ethnographers and politicians, rather than by jurists or bureaucrats. This explains why in these regions language has become synonymous with ethnicity, or with the nation or state. Cultural and political theorists must use this as a starting point when considering the formation of collective identity. Starting with Germany, whose historical evolution is interlinked with that of Central Europe, and moving on to Romania, Bulgaria, Serbia or Greece – all of which have been strongly influenced by the German cultural model – the championing of the theory of ethnicity is based on imaginary constructs and the dismissal of accurate historical facts, placing itself in direct contrast to the values of the modern European state. Germany's rebirth after the Second World War illustrates how essential it is to escape the grip of this old ideology. In Germany, the revival of local cultural heritage, coupled with American influence and support (economic and otherwise), has played a vital role in transforming its culture, society and politics.

In the regions where language, ethnography, geography and religion are allowed to define national identity, differentialism born in the Romantic era threatens to take root. In some countries, only one of the aforementioned regional characteristics takes on a powerful significance and becomes the defining factor of nationality. Collective identity is an attractive prospect for many, but when it threatens individual conscience this identity becomes meaningless, as its sole value is as a gateway to social emancipation. We have already seen how the transition from medieval social and political structures to the modern world created a crisis that led some to search for ideologies that consolidated collective identity.

2. SYMBOLIC FIGURES AND ROMANIAN CONCEPTUAL CONFUSIONS

Aside from the actual content of texts, there is a fundamental breakdown of communication between writers and their audiences. In regions where there is a large middle class, the elites have no one to engage in dialogue. As a result, they become convinced that their role is simply to emote rather than communicate constructive ideas. It is these elites – individuals who control language and are in full possession of the facts – who shape a community's social aspirations, but instead of encouraging change in social behaviour, they possess a dangerous predilection for abstractions. In Romanian culture, for instance, the use of the terms kin, ethnicity and people reveals a bias towards symbolic language versus an attempt to re-organise social structures. This illustrates the way that the concept of nation can take on a dimension that completely ignores the concrete significance of the individual or society, just one step away from totalitarianism. In nineteenth-century Romania, this kind of discourse was used continually by the aristocracy and later by the middle classes. These intellectuals sought to protect the privileges of the social system that gave them status. Their ideas did not reflect a social doctrine bearing any resemblance to that of Jules Michelet and his contemporaries. Instead, they were seduced by a messianic version of history, one that, in conjunction with the Church, sought to bring about the first emancipation of the masses. Such elements could not foster the kind of balanced mentality that would steer their societies towards modernisation. This trend was most visible in Romania.

The social realities of the country were exposed after 1918 and, as a result, there was support for introducing a state programme for the emancipation of Romanians living in Transylvania, Banat, Bucovina and Bessarabia. The experiences of intellectuals from the Old Kingdom is particularly interesting because some of them took on administrative positions in Transylvania. They noted the inferiority complex felt by Romanians who lived alongside Germans and Hungarians, and the way this led to educational reforms. Despite the fact that Romanian schools were fairly common, they were overshadowed by institutions founded by the German and Hungarian communities. According to some historical sources, this imbalance persisted even after those territories were controlled by the Romanian authorities. An inspection report from 1926 in the county of Târnava Mică concluded:

We are presented with two, entirely different, worlds; one of them is ruled by light, the other one by darkness; one is wealthy, the other is poor; one is chaotic, the other orderly and disciplined. How could the Germans and the Romanians live together side by side for so many centuries without the latter being positively influenced by the former?[9]

The inspector's description is regrettable but accurate. He noticed not only that the German community functioned effectively, but also why it operated more effectively than the Romanian community. Unfortunately, intellectuals could not – and still cannot – provide a satisfactory answer to the inspector's question and have ignored any possible solutions to these educational deficiencies.

Another important aspect was the lack of interaction between the Romanian-German and the rural communities. As the inspector implied, these were two worlds based on different values. In Transylvania, they were closed communities that had remained unchanged since the Middle Ages. Even though Romanians lived side by side with the German minority, they did not share the same values. The Romanian population was urbanised later than the German community, impeding its social mobility and cultural emancipation. These shortcomings, coupled with slow economic development, disadvantaged the Romanian masses and negatively affected the establishment of social institutions. However, the dysfunctional relationship between different communities in Transylvania was caused mostly by those who stoked conflict to protect the interests of their own ethnic group.

There was an opportunity in 1918 to re-evaluate history and create bridges between the Romanian, German and Hungarian communities. Unfortunately, instead of steering the country in a liberal direction, the ruling elites in Bucharest and other administrative regional centres opted for a conservative ideology that deepened these divisions. Sorin Alexandrescu writes:

> By opting for a more centrist political path that focused on cooperation there could have been a way of attenuating these differences. It was necessary to establish a unified educational system and to provide Romanian schools in regions that fell under Hungarian or Russian administration. However, the post-war governments did not consider the long-term effect of favouring this educational system.[10]

At the same time as politicians imposed this forced centralisation, intellectuals did not fully engage with the problems faced by Romanian society. They did not acknowledge the fact that by adopting this collectivist position, Romania was moving in a different direction from the rest of the world. Individualism was sacrificed at the expense of a collectivist philosophy favoured by a dominant minority. Accustomed as they were to evaluating society from their own preferred perspective or through the prism of rigid ideologies, Romanian intellectuals did not address the concerns of the masses with an open mind. For them, it was essential to revive the historical myth of the nineteenth century in order to strengthen national identity. The political changes following the First World War did not temper their ideological excesses or manage to repair the social ruptures from the previous century. The centralism of the Romanian administration failed to capitalise on newly acquired state resources and use them to create economic stability. Instead, with the help of these intellectuals, it fuelled the ideology of the superiority or inferiority of different groups.

Constantin Noica and his peers created a whole philosophy based on collectivism. Noica wrote:

> Political revolutions are not made by and for the few, but with the participation of many. For an organism to be healthy, all its organs need to be in good shape. What did the Legion want? It desired a new soul for the country. For centuries – yes, maybe for centuries – a few graves can sustain the soul of the country. But today the country demands another body. The new soul of the country demands a body to match it. All of us, who are its members – do we not decide on its health? If one of us is rotten, the body suffers... Do you want life for the Romanian people? Look at it in the sun tomorrow. It came to meet yours, which has not yet gone out into the sun...[11]

Matters relating to individual consciousness have often been sidestepped in Romanian public life. Instead, leading philosophers and historians have championed the idea of a centralised culture. According to Ernest Gellner, this is a reaction against the peasantry rather than a celebration of their culture. Nationalist symbolism is closely linked to their old traditions and the vigour of rural life, which is associated with Volk or kin. However, once urbanised, these peasants did not have a say in the direction that this national culture would take.[12] The concepts of ethnicity reflected the primordial, instinctive rural way of life, which is why they were of particular interest to the nationalists.

Many historians, claiming to investigate the past and the concepts that shaped it, are still fascinated by the ethnonational dimension of political states. Keith Hitchins claims that the ethnic nation is a modern concept. This idea is echoed by Romanian histo-riographers, but is somewhat surprising to hear from an American.[13] This correlation between ethnicity and language leads me to believe that it is necessary to analyse the nature of cultural and political dis-course. The study of the concepts used to define collectivity enables us to understand political practices. For many generations, whenever historians, linguists, ethnographers and politicians have discussed the topic of identity they have used and misused terminology derived from the Romantic era, when group identity was first celebrated.

The Romanian conceptions of kin, ethnicity, people and natio-nality illustrate the attempt of a culture to create specific terms to define its identity. This form of identity – amplified for the benefit of the masses through various cultural and political tools – created problems for ethnic minorities in the nineteenth century, namely the marginalisation of groups who did not speak Romanian as their mother tongue and those who were not in the Orthodox majority. In short, it was a highly subjective interpretation of the concept of the nation. Even today, language and religion are used to create distinctions between groups and often lead to discrimination. Even if we accept the reasons behind ethnonationalism at a particular historical period when the idea of nation was conceived, it seems unacceptable that it should be passed on uncritically from one generation to the next.

The terms kin, ethnicity, people and nationality are inter-linked and became embedded in political ideologies in regions where a sense of national consciousness developed later – for example Germany, Poland, the Czech Republic, Serbia and Romania – where they were stimulated by the absence of an organised state.[14] Andrei Cornea argues that only 'nationalism takes the idea of people (kin, das Volk) symbolically and adapts it into concepts which eventu-ally oppose their literal meanings: nationalism equates people with ethnicity, which implies that it must rid itself of other ethnic minori-ties'.[15] Although this description accurately describes the Romanian context, there are certain details that distinguish these terms from those used in other languages and cultures.

Nowadays, studies relating to Begriffsgeschichte and the history of concepts have revealed the way the connotations of terms differ according to cultural context. When we discuss the notion of people as in the French *peuple* or the Anglo-American people, we have a different understanding according to the nature of those societies and populations, as the meaning of these terms is intimately connected with legal ideas about *citoyenneté* or citizenship. In those cultures, the terms symbolise specific institutions that define the social and civic status of their citizens. *Peuple* or people are the totality of all the individuals in those states. In Romanian, people becomes *popor*, a term whose connotations also vary according to the perspective of the person using it, a word which acquires different nuances at specific political moments. When used in a revolutionary sense, it is coloured by French connotations of economic justice and the status of the masses.

For a brief period in 1848, intellectuals from Wallachia were concerned with creating a national identity that would benefit the country's entire population. In Transylvania, however – with some exceptions, notably Alexandru Papiu Ilarian – the leaders' conception of this identity was not based on juridical structures. Instead, in this region, the rhetoric regarding nationhood focused on origins, bloodlines and connection to the earth. Paul Cornea argues that there was a conflict between the realistic and idealised visions of *popor*, but that Romanian intellectuals in 1848 understood the different connotations of *plebs* and *populus*.[16]

I believe that in Central and Eastern European culture this political terminology was ambiguous rather than precise. For example, a few years later, the Romanian *popor* becomes synonymous with *kin*, which in turn takes on the meaning of *ethnicity* but also *nation*, in the sense that it refers to a community that shares the same bloodlines, culture and language in a particular geographical space. The result was a *Kulturnation* inspired by the Romantic *Volk* rather than a political structure based on the values and laws implied by the concepts of *peuple* or people.

Apart from the aforementioned exception in Wallachia, I have not come across *popor* being used in the sense of *populus* (as a political and juridical community). Since then, political language and collective consciousness have not evolved in that direction, which is one of the reasons why the civic-liberal and leftist positions have been inconsistently represented in Romanian culture. In the absence of the culture of *populus*, *peuple* or people, a tribal national identity was formed. Despite some similarities, there are significant differences between the Romanian idea of kin (often equated with people) and the manifestation of such concepts in French, English or Dutch cultures.

3. THE RACIAL CONNOTATIONS OF KIN

If the French influence was still felt in the regions that were once part of the Old Kingdom of Romania, such as Wallachia and Moldova, even after the 1848 revolution, the German influence on Transylvania lasted longer still. Looking at the work of Petru Maior and his disciples, it is possible to observe the evolution of the concept of kin, which was associated by the Transylvanian School (Școala ardeleană) with ethnic purity, and the role it played in Romania's attempt to define its identity in the nineteenth century. Timotei Cipariu remarked that 'Romanians have never approved of foreign blood mixing with their own. This is just as true nowadays as it has been in the past, and there is no reason to persuade them otherwise.'[17] Gheorghe Barițiu was convinced that the Romanian peasant 'couldn't stand the idea of his sons interbreeding, or even changing their traditional dress'.[18] These views were supported by Damaschin Bojincă and Moise Nicoară, both of whom were obsessed with the idea of racial purity. On the other hand, academics such as Paul Iorgovici saw the benefits of mixing cultures.

According to researchers, mixed marriages were discouraged in the communities of Transylvania and Banat. There are various theories as to why this might have been the case, but none is satisfactory. This does not seem to have been the result of an identity crisis specific to the beginning of the modern era, as Sorin Mitu suggests, but a feature of the culture and political thinking of Romanian communities during the nineteenth and twentieth centuries. This culture was not confined to Transylvania. This identity crisis intensified from the end of the nineteenth century through to the interwar period, especially as a result of the Fascist and Communist dictatorships. These regimes triggered a loss of confidence in this national identity and stimulated nationalist rhetoric. The existence of successful intercultural communities in Banat, Bucovina, Crișana,

Dobrogea and Maramureş has not significantly corrected the proliferation of stereotypes in the Romanian collective imagination.

Furthermore, the work of Vasile Conta and Aurel C. Popovici also reflects the racial subtext of the concepts of people-kin-ethnicity-nationality. In his historical studies, Conta proclaimed his belief that a people were united by race and that this race was fundamental to their identity. He believed this applied to both the Romanian and the Jewish races – both had to remain separate and distinct in order to preserve their identity, hence his comments on 'the Jewish question':

> The Jews are a separate nation and the enemy of all the others... we might say that the nation of the Jews is the most distinct and stable in the whole world. This is because they have retained the most important aspect of a nation – racial purity.

Conta maintained that all members of a people have the same blood coursing through their veins, and this, he seems to imply, would ensure that they all shared the same faith, feelings and ideas. Conta's aim was to persuade his readers that a nation and a state must be built on racial purity. In this way, kin-ethnicity-nation are equated with race. His theory reveals a nostalgia for an archaic, peasant culture. Conta's ideal of Romanian identity could only be realised if members of different ethnic groups did not marry outside their communities, so as to preserve racial purity.[19]

Popovici campaigned for the Austro-Hungarian Empire to be federalised on the basis of kin. His book *Die Vereinigten Staaten von Groß-Österreich. Politische Studien zur Lösung der nationalen Fragen und Staatsrechtlichen Krisen in Österreich-Ungarn* (*The United States of Greater Austria: Political Studies on the Solution to National Questions and Constitutional Crises in Austria-Hungary*) promotes this type of biological racism: 'When analysing any successful nation, we see that its population retained its distinct character and did not mix. Even zoology teaches us that when animals interbreed they produce offspring without any true character.' Elsewhere, he writes:

> In order to create a superior nation, intermarriage must not occur, as it dilutes the bloodline and ethnic traditions. Gobineau was the first to point out the effect of this on

civilisation and the way it can lead to the pure essence of certain peoples disappearing. According to him, this would never happen without interbreeding.

Popovici sees people, ethnicity and race as interconnected. As well as 'interbreeding', he also considers that the introduction of civil marriage in the Austro-Hungarian Empire at the end of the nineteenth century led to racial degeneration, claiming that 'all great nations have avoided ethnic assimilation'.[20] Popovici elaborated on the ethnonationalist and racial arguments presented in *Essai sur l'inégalité des races humaines* (*Essay on the Inequality of Races*) by Gobineau and *Die Grundlagen des Neunzehnten Jahrhundert* (*The Foundations of the Nineteenth Century*) by Houston Stewart Chamberlain. Although inspired by these works, he went a step further and used them as the basis of a nationalism founded on racial superiority. This becomes clear from his definition of nationalism, which he describes as 'the sense of superiority to other nations' and 'the battle to assert this superiority'.[21]

His understanding of kin as interrelated to people-ethnicity-race is similar to the German concept of *Volk* in that it implies discrimination. Popovici's ideas have been very influential in Romanian culture and public life, but they have rarely been properly analysed or decoded. This is one of the reasons why the country has struggled to formulate a national identity that suits modern Europe. According to linguist Alexandru Niculescu, common use of the term kin reflects a cultural inclination to see people and nation as linked. This inclination seems out of kilter with modern thinking, making it all the more remarkable: 'So, are we to see kin, as N. Iorga argued, as exclusively Romanian, Christian, Orthodox, meaning that all other elements of Romanian society – other ethnicities, religions – are not part of our Kin?'[22] Alexandru Niculescu's question illustrates the importance of redefining history and the political language used to express Romanian culture and identity. This is a vital task if we are to free ourselves of this conservative mentality.

The concept of kin entered the political language of Romania in the twentieth century. In one of his articles, which he also used as the basis for lectures, historian Nicolae Iorga writes about the Transylvanian School:

All their arguments about the nobility and characteristics of kin were taken from books, but they could have been observed in real life, the same truth could have been discovered by investigating the origins of this kin, which so far have not been adequately explored; they could have highlighted the unity of kin by showing how it manifested itself in the traditions of the people and their art.[23]

Iorga felt that the concept of kin had to be connected to the masses as well as to ancestral traditions. However, the desire to revive this glorious past creates a parallel between Iorga's theories and those of the Transylvanian School. This common point of reference reveals the way that the concept of kin is used to create a particular type of national identity. Passed down through the generations, the myth of pure origins becomes more and more potent in discussions of the past, present and future of Romanian society.

As Iorga's words illustrate, the concept of kin was a point of discussion in the Old Kingdom of Romania, where it was connected with tradition, ethnicity and Orthodoxism. Eventually, kin became exclusively associated with ethnicity. For Iorga, kin simultaneously signified nation and race. During this time, several Romanian intellectuals and publications remarked on the 'dangerous theories' of nationalism. Some of Iorga's contemporaries expressed their concerns in the newspaper *Acțiunea* (*Action*) about this 'hostility towards different social classes and races' as well as his supporters' contempt for the rule of law.

Iorga, considered Romania's foremost historiographer, popularised the racist interpretation of kin. Unfortunately, his influence ensured that these ideas were passed on uncritically for decades. In one of many examples in which he expresses such views he states: 'Let us create political platforms that champion our unique and precious kin. Let us discard the borrowed rags that do not fit us and stand in the way of our development.' Differentialism becomes the organic product of a philosophy focused on otherness. Iorga feels that the national body must be stripped of this ill-fitting cloth to be purified and for the community to become united. This dream 'has not yet been realised, but it must be sown in every individual's consciousness'.[24] When describing Romania's neighbours, he also refs to their race: 'In medieval Hungary... there was no sense of national identity, as the Pope simply bestowed a Byzantine crown upon its ruler with the purpose of promoting Catholicism rather than Hungarian culture. If only the current generation of Hungarians would realise this, we would be happy to extend to them a hand of friendship and help them develop their nation in a direction suited to their race.'[25]

Iorga was the forerunner of a generation of intellectuals who overlooked the problems faced by Romanians and other ethnic communities within the Old Kingdom, Transylvania, Banat, Crișana and Maramureș. His ideas about origins would garner support and encounter opposition. Nae Ionescu, the mentor of Romania's Fascist Iron Guard, made the following claim for Iorga's ideas:

> In 'The Sower', Iorga was the first to lay down the foundations of Romanian civilisation. His temperament and spiritual purpose were unparalleled. His work revealed to us that the only hope for the revival of the Romanian state and civilisation was autochthonism, meaning that we should prize everything distinctly Romanian and gain our spiritual nourishment from the peasant class.[26]

Alexandru C. Cuza, Mihail Manoilescu, Mihail Polihroniade, Nichifor Crainic, Radu Gyr and Dan Botta continued on the same theme, putting even more emphasis on the problems of otherness, minorities and Jews. They would use the concept of kin with its connotations of race to emphasise the division between Romanians and Hungarians, Germans, Russians and Jews to create the image of a distinct, unified Romanian consciousness. In this context, kin took on the same semantic nuances as *Volk*, although it did not have the same complex meaning. One of the staunchest proponents of this theory of collective identity was Cuza, a close associate of Nicolae Iorga in the early twentieth century: 'Nationality is a natural, organic, spiritual force born out of blood ties. A unified race is full of positive qualities which are lost through interbreeding and degenerate, rendering it sterile and enfeebled.' Elsewhere, Cuza writes: 'The nation is comprised of individuals that share the same blood, which creates a collective consciousness brought to life by the natural vigour of nationality tied to a common land, creating living, productive organisms.'[27]

Those who created racist laws under the dictatorships that emerged during the reigns of Carol II and Ion Antonescu were not only inspired by Nazism. As we can see from the passages above, there were plenty of other sources to help them develop an idea of the nation. The concept of kin, with its racist connotations, played an important role in promoting discrimination, xenophobia and anti-Semitism. This was the rhetoric used by Ion Antonescu's regime. Transnistria was chosen as one of the regions where the purification of kin would be carried out. Although it did not reach the same level as the Nazis, Antonescu's regime carried out mass killings motivated by racism.

The leaders of the Antonescu regime were keen to promote a doctrine based on biological origin. Here are two such statements that reflect the influences on Antonescu's political thinking:

> This is how I was brought up, with a hatred towards the Turks, the Jews and the Hungarians. We have to take this hatred towards the enemies of the country to the extreme. I will take on this responsibility...[28]

> If we do not take advantage of the national and European situation at the moment then we will miss the last chance history has given us to purify the Romanian kin... even if we gain Bessarabia and Transylvania, we would have achieved nothing if we do not cleanse our kin, because it is not dependent on geographical borders, but on the homogeneity and purity of the race. And this is my ultimate goal.[29]

This racist doctrine asserts that the most important component of an individual or a group is its blood. His speeches to the Council of Ministers make it clear that Antonescu considers purification of kin as fundamental to establishing the state, a racist ideology which has parallels to the Nazi regime.

The concept of kin remained a part of the national consciousness under Communism. During Ceauşescu's dictatorship, it was present in different forms – in literary life, historical studies, folklore, popular music and everyday language. Historiographers continued to promote ethnocultural differentialism or neotribalism (Karl Popper's term). In comparison with previous eras it was less extreme, but retained its archaic value and remained a powerful force in the public sphere. Since 1989, it has been part of the cultural, religious and political language.

As Romania is a democratic country that wants to be further integrated into the pluralist European Union, the concept of kin is a dangerous one, and while some of its promoters might not fully comprehend its implications, it is used by religious ideologues whose purpose is to revive ethnonationalism. Unlike the concepts of people, ethnicity, nationality and nation, the idea of kin has not been sufficiently analysed from the perspective of the history of ideas. In this respect, we have fallen behind other European political bodies. It would be a mistake to assume that this matter is irrelevant to many citizens and that ethnonationalist discourse can therefore be used without repercussions. This is yet another reason why Romanian identity should be analysed from an academic point of view, rather than simply remain part of propaganda.

The arguments I have presented in this section are similar to those formulated by Professor Alexandru Niculescu in relation to kin in Hungary. He considers the term *nem*, which implies sex or type, and in academic language points to category or species. The Hungarian *nem* is part of the words *nemes* (noble, generous) and *nemzet* (national community).[30] As far as the word for kin in Romanian is concerned (*neam*), it appeared first in Transylvania, borrowed from Hungarian, which had been the region's official language for a long time. Aside from the traditional, Orthodox and autochthonous dimensions identified by Alexandru Niculescu, I am certain that in the Romanian language kin is related to the concepts of ethnicity-nationality-nation and that, in certain contexts, it is synonymous with people. The Transylvanian School saw it as intricately tied to the ancient rural world, to the earth (*jus solis*) and to blood ties (*jus sanguinis*), and therefore these connotations passed into academic and religious discourse.

It should be noted that in the rural world, kin is understood to denote family, local and tribal relationships. For the peasants, kin meant consanguinity. The racist connotations became inseparable from political ideology, transmitted through oral and written culture and promoted first by Transylvanian Romanians and later by members of the Old Kingdom of Romania. German Romanticism also played a part in endowing the word with these nuances. The German equivalent of tribe or kin is *der Stamm*. *Das Volk* is a combination of people and kin. The pairing of kin-nation – like *Volk*-nation – reveals the development of Romanian revolutionary discourse at the time when the nation state was formed. In a different era, it could be seen as a concept that fuelled an exclusivist ideology. In both instances, its champions created their ideal by merging biology with political thinking.

V
THEORETICAL ANALYSIS OF THE ROMANIAN CONCEPT OF NATION

1. HOSTILITY TOWARDS DIVERSITY OR THE FANTASY OF THE ORGANIC NATION

The concept of nation was first formulated in the nineteenth century, and it is remarkable how many ideologues have offered different perspectives on this subject over time. It has been an important topic of discussion in many fields: history, religion, linguistics, ethnography, philosophy, sociology, statistics, law, anthropology and geography. The concept of nation was seen not only as the myth that would create a unified, common identity, but also as a great political achievement. Recent sociological and historical research has drawn attention to the cultural and political connotations with which this notion has been invested over the past two centuries. Some studies have analysed the works that have dealt with this ideology and investigated their writers' motivations. Others have focused on the challenges faced by academics in formulating a theory of national unification, considering the Romanian state formed in 1918 comprised regions with a diverse cultural heritage and different institutions and religious practices.

A third group has analysed the impact of nationalism on minority groups at the end of the nineteenth century and during the interwar years. Finally, still others researched the extent to which the concept of the Romanian nation is a mythical construct, similar to other such cases in Central, Eastern and Southeastern Europe.[1]

Earlier in this book, I decoded the notions of kin and people, focusing on sources from the nineteenth and twentieth centuries. My intention was to expose the shortcomings of these terms in defining collective Romanian identity and to reflect on the relationship between kin and nation or people and nation. In this chapter, I shall turn my attention to the social, elitist and cultural dimensions of the concept of nation, along with the self-defeating qualities of this ideology formulated by nineteenth-century intellectuals. I will consider the theory of identity that prevails in Romanian society; in other words, the fictive ethnicity used by elites as the basis of nationalism.[2]

When Titu Maiorescu talked about empty forms, structural heterogeneity and the logic of bipolarity in relation to Romanian political culture, he was drawing a comparison between Romania and the West. Maiorescu was trying to find a solution to the disequilibrium previously mentioned in relation to the principles on which the modern nation was founded. He was concerned that the transition of the Romanian state from the medieval to the modern era was too slow. For a long time, two completely different forms of organisation and ways of life coexisted within Romanian society: on the one hand there was the collective, medieval structure of the rural world, while on the other there was the bourgeois individualism that dominated urban society. This state of affairs contributed to the development of a philosophy that privileged the old aristocratic elite. This elitist model survives today, as seen in higher education, politics and culture. The differentialist and essentialist ideas that gave rise to discrimination and corruption are still influential. Leaders need to maintain the existing social hierarchy rather than seek to elevate the masses and transform them into social and civic equals.

For example, Nae Ionescu – a famous philosophy professor at the University of Bucharest during the 1930s and spiritual father of the Iron Guard – saw people as an organic unity, an amorphous spiritual mass whose members lacked an individual consciousness, from which no remarkable personalities had emerged. He stated:

Within a nation, it is not necessary for everyone to be involved in politics as this is not their given role. A nation must function politically, but only some are required to engage in political thought and action. Why? Because only those with a clear understanding of what this nation means are capable of acting in its interests.[3]

The masses had to obey the decisions of the elite, no matter how subjective or callous these decisions might be. Nae Ionescu displayed 'an elitist contempt' here, irrationally favouring the judgements of the leaders over those of the masses.[4]

A similar sentiment was conveyed by the poet Dan Botta, who stated that ignorance and illiteracy were preferable to learning, social pluralism or freedom of expression:

> Let us be clear. We have adopted Western norms, such as their mania for technology and so-called democratic ideals. We have turned into a herd, and dark monsters prey on our factories. But this is not the Romanian way. As I have said many times, those people are made up of rods and levers, they are purely mechanical, susceptible to either good or evil. They are all identical. Their schools are designed to create uniformity, to make them forget their past, their heredity. Romanians are different. They have created the most noble folklore, their spirit is infinitely complex, they are the ancient shepherds, spiritual people, possessing the Platonic 'sensitive soul' that transcends space and time, and yet these people have had their uniqueness stripped away from them by education… They have had to learn by rote the muddled phrases and ideas of foreign cultures infinitely inferior to their own. Romanian education has adopted Western principles to oppress and destroy the Romanian soul… illiteracy would be preferable to this.[5]

Emil Cioran held similar anti-democratic beliefs, expressing his contempt and prejudice towards the peasantry in an article entitled 'Renouncing Liberty':

Whoever knows anything about our peasantry, with their simple, rudimentary mentality, will understand that they need to be freed from the illusion of liberty. They are crying out for a real dictatorship and hate this useless freedom. For those who are not the makers of history there is nothing. Democracy has given them an active role in history, but their eternal ignorance makes them uninterested in it. The peasants want everything to be decided for them, therefore dictatorship is their ideal system... These masses, cut off from history, have only one aspiration: to give up their freedom. They want others to take responsibility; they do not want to think for themselves and are terrified of anarchy. Anyway, a society without despotic leaders would soon turn to cannibalism and self-destruct. Freedom is the most overrated of all human values.[6]

Many intellectuals in the interwar era (and since) have shared these opinions. This prejudiced view that supported the inherited social hierarchy was a feature of both Fascist and Communist thinking. These ideas were passed on through family generations, education and society. Some echoes of it have resurfaced in the post-Communist world. Adrian-Paul Iliescu argues that the present obsession with elitism is not inspired by the sort of ideas that underpinned the Legionarism of the Iron Guard, as it is neither anti-Semitic nor Fascistic. It does, however, share some elements of the interwar Far Right as it sees the elite as special and aspiring towards a uniform social landscape: 'In other words, while it does not directly affiliate itself with Legionarism, the present-day obsession with the elites reflects a hostility towards diversity.'[7] This remark is important as it highlights the recurrence of these principles at various stages in Romanian history. In turn, it raises the question of whether it is this Romanian mentality or quasi-Oriental notions borrowed from elsewhere that have prevented them from fully adopting Western values.

This melange of values and ideologies over time has distanced Romania from Western civilisation. To be more precise, it has allowed the peasantry and urban population during the nineteenth and twentieth centuries to cling to outdated values and ignore advances in science, technology, administration and law that have had a major impact on the rest of the modern world. Those who have attempted to broaden its cultural horizons, reinterpret folkloric traditions and modernise villages have been met with resistance. It seems to me that we should focus not only on existing traditions that have survived, but also on what has been lost as a consequence of trying to preserve archaic values – namely, modernisation and Westernisation. In 1938, only 4 million out of 18 million Romanian citizens were urban dwellers. Then, as is the case now, villages suffered from worse living conditions than towns and cities. The peasantry – which still constitutes between 35 and 38 per cent of the Romanian population – had limited access to education due to the fact that there were few schools in the countryside. It certainly was not the case that the existence of these schools had an adverse impact on the rural population, as Dan Botta had claimed. Availability of healthcare was also insufficient. Between 1930 and 1940, in the region south of the Carpathians there was reportedly only one doctor for every 25 villages.

Access to urban centres remained difficult in the decades following the Second World War. These were some of the reasons Romania lagged behind Europe on many fronts. The development of rural areas was halted by a lack of resources and the unwillingness of leaders to deal with the disparity between social classes. The lack of political and social power of many regions in Romania has resulted in the development of social groups whose discourse and mentality differs from those of the modern world. The pseudo-emancipation engineered by the post-war Communist regime led to the ruralisation of towns rather than the urbanisation of villages. This phenomenon had significant cultural implications. Often, rather than constructing a civil society, totalitarian regimes revived a traditionalist culture, such as ethnonationalism. Founded by a fragmented, self-elected elite and a self-serving political class that turned its back on social pedagogy, the nation state created by Romanian intellectuals in the nineteenth and twentieth centuries took on an organic quality unknown in Western political culture. Instead of trying to implement principles that would benefit the whole community, the education system favoured the elites. Meanwhile, the rhetoric of collectivism continued to dominate – 'masses... have only one single aspiration: to give up their freedom', as Cioran put it – at the expense of individualism. All these factors led to the rejection of Western European values and to the formation of a nation that had not reaped the rewards of the Enlightenment, as it turned its back on reform and innovation.

Besides the geographical and political context (often mythologised) and poverty, we must take into account the differences in language and behaviour between the majority of Romanian society and other European states, and the role of the intelligentsia in deepening these divisions. Even today, we see this sector of Romanian society arrogantly dismissing or belittling Western values. Their position is not only unproductive but irrational. This sense of superiority was nurtured by the education and culture of totalitarian regimes and has prevented them from fully engaging with the problem of European integration.

Twentieth-century intellectuals such as Aurel C. Popovici,[8] Constantin Noica[9] and Nicolae Iorga[10] did not necessarily ignore the difference between the patriarchal, medieval society and the modern one, but their understanding of the idea of nation was based on sentimental-Romantic and traditionalist-conservative historiography and philosophy from the nineteenth century. Their vision was too narrow because it was tied to elitism and the uncritical adoption of concepts that had been migrating to Eastern Europe from the West since the eighteenth century. They were seduced by the idea that the Romanian nation was essentially linked to an ethnicity that had survived since time immemorial and needed to be led by the genius of the intellectual elite. Romanian culture has been caught in two traps: it overestimated the role of collectivism (which inhibited emancipation) and gave too much power to certain boyar families, whose descendants still make up the revered intellectual and political classes. Similar problems can be seen in nearby countries such as the former Yugoslavia and Albania, where conflicting ideologies have had tragic consequences, which suggests that it is important to examine the way collective identity has been defined in Central, Eastern and Southeastern Europe.

A small ethnic group's fetishisation of the concepts of nation and nation state is not only fantastical but harmful, as it creates artificial divisions within societies based on language and religious beliefs. Furthermore, this myth and the discourse associated with it ignore social reality and assert there is some kind of tribal bond within a group created by blood ties, language and religious faith. After 1989, minority groups in Romania were sometimes tempted to adopt the same ideology of identity, leading to a conflict of interests as the minorities challenged political structures that did not seem to represent them. These minorities, such as the Hungarian community, campaigned for a multinational state, challenging the monocultural orientation of Romanian society. For these reasons, every discussion on the topic of the nation must take into account the social, linguistic and cultural diversity in Romania born out of its tumultuous history. Those who claim that the Orthodox religion is Romanian and should dominate public space should remember that it is also a faith shared by the Slavs south of the Danube, the Greeks, the Ukrainians and the Russians, and that Romanians are not only Orthodox but also Catholic, Protestant, neo-Protestant and Jewish. In reality, the Romanian nation is richly diverse, just like the rest of Central, Eastern and Southeastern Europe.

2. REFUSAL OF DISCONTINUITY, OR THE CONFUSION BETWEEN THE OLD PATRIARCHAL SOCIETY AND THE MODERN NATION: A NEO-ROMANTIC PERSPECTIVE ON THE BEGINNINGS OF THE ROMANIAN NATION

The supporters of ethnocracy not only ignore the modernisation of urban society but claim that there exists an essential collective being. Nichifor Crainic, whose arguments are fantastical rather than empirical, states that in Romania's history there have been remarkable personalities who possessed 'ethnic genius', embodied moral discipline and furthered the ultimate goals of the state:

> When we think of those wills so much stronger than our own, hearts of unparalleled heroism, our souls are touched by the power of the Romanian spirit. This will be the epoch of the ethnic state, proclaimed by the thunderous voices of the omnipotent, the state where the borders of our country will be the borders of blood...

Crainic and his followers saw the state as defined by a collective identity created on the basis of ethnicity, one built on racism and biology: 'The unique and all-encompassing experience of life within the state is fundamental to nationalism and imprints the ideal of the nation in the souls of its citizens.' Public life will be governed by an authoritarian regime and the individual will become just one molecule of the larger collective.[11] This rhetoric privileges the 'we' as opposed to the 'I', with responsibility transferred from the individual to the group. This freedom from responsibility cancels the individual's right to independent thought, allowing the intellectual elite to make all decisions. The result, as Kant argued, is the population's eventual fear of thinking for themselves. Crainic's ideas were echoed by almost all intellectuals active in the interwar period, many of whom continued to propagate this ideology during the years of Communist dictatorship. This explains the popularity of the concept of an ethnonational culture.

Those who have studied social structures in Romania have commented on the way the myth of rural life has been used as a tool to create a political and cultural atmosphere that benefited those already in positions of power. The intellectual elite disseminated ideas about traditions and roots that assert the right of the original inhabitants, their common blood ties and bond to the earth. Following in Iorga's footsteps, this generation would proclaim that 'Romania belongs to the Romanians, to all Romanians and only to the Romanians'.

Both after the First World War and during the Communist period following the Second World War, a number of academics clung to this view and refused to renounce it even after it was clear that it opposed the European values shared by some of their peers.[12] Even the Marxism-Leninism imposed by the Soviets was superseded by the theory of re-autochthonisation. Between 1970 and 1990, the Romanian intelligentsia drew inspiration from Constantin Noica. Post-war protochronism, which mirrored the perspective of the interwar generation, returned to the theme of the supremacy of quintessential Romanian culture. Such anti-Western ideas were not tested through critical evaluation. Instead, they aligned themselves with the ideology of differentialist ethnonationalism. According to Zigu Ornea and Adrian Marino, the post-war nationalism of Nichifor

Crainic and Nae Ionescu was revived under Ceauşescu's leadership. Both of these manifestations of the same doctrine were 'united through the merging of vision and faith'.[13]

Romanian intellectuals who respect modern European values point out the harmful impact of historical doctrines that refuse to engage with new perspectives. Writing at the end of the nineteenth century and the beginning of the twentieth, Titu Maiorescu, C. D. Zeletin and Eugen Lovinescu believed that Romania's integration in Europe was possible. They understood that what mattered was not only historical, traditional, religious and linguistic continuity, but also structural reform, the dynamics of social relationships and the modernisation of rural culture. In their view, the new nation had to abandon its medieval way of life and take new risks. Although they faced opposition from many celebrated cultural figures, their project was worth pursuing.

According to the research of Keith Hitchins, Imre Pászka, Zigu Ornea, Irina Livezeanu, Vladimir Tismăneanu and George Voicu, there was a crisis in national identity after 1918 that promoted intellectual debate about the creation of a new administrative and cultural order. Ethnocentrist-nationalist academics were suspicious of the integration of Romania into the European community. The 1930s and 1940s saw a revival of Orthodoxism and an ethnonation ideal that needed to purge itself of all foreign elements, including existing minority groups. This idea took on a mystical quality that to some extent still lingers. Orthodoxism was seen as synonymous with the Romanian spirit and antagonistic to Western influences, hence it became the key point of reference in public discourse. Nae Ionescu and Nichifor Crainic's notion of the Romanian spirit was intertwined with Orthdoxism, and any other religious faith was seen as alien and unpatriotic. 'To be a Romanian, not a good Romanian, simply a Romanian,' Nae Ionescu writes, 'you have to be Orthodox.'[14] Elsewhere, he also comments on the relationship between nationality and the Orthodox faith:

> Our natures are determined by the structure of the community to which we belong. In other words, history chronicles the way that nations, rather than individual lives, evolve and are shaped by the word God. This is why faithfulness to

the Church has to be part of a nation's destiny. This is what Orthodoxism stands for.[15]

Even if some of our institutions and laws regarding minorities have adapted to European standards and we see economic progress in the larger cities, rural Romania is still in thrall to the old ways inherited from a semi-Orientalist, Turkish-Phanariot culture. The regression of Romania during the interwar era was not due to the lack of an autochthonous bourgeoisie, but was the result of a culture and a social pedagogy focused on abstract nationalist ideals that ignored social, cultural and religious realities. Communitarianism was given a voice by the interwar media and culminated in the discriminatory biological ideas that dominated public life in the 1940s. Aside from the unjust segregation it caused, this movement was also to blame for hindering social emancipation, despite the cultural progress made during the reign of Carol I. Any political progress during that era was undermined by the rhetoric of nationalism that invoked the old patriarchal society.

Why did the Romanian intelligentsia choose to inhabit this atemporal space? What is the connection between the cultural and the national perspective and to what extent does politics undermine the creative-scientific approach? Why were so many seduced by the idea of the ethnonationalist community? Why have the works of Nicolae Iorga, Nae Ionescu, Nichifor Crainic or Constantin Noica, which made only general links between Romanian culture and politics, continued to be seen as the key texts of post-war culture? One researcher who investigated these questions argued that 'the shift from the ontological (relating to being) to the ontic (relating to being-community-nationality) created an ambivalence that persisted in Romanian politics and culture'.[16] This statement sheds light on the problems of being-community-nationality both in the interwar and post-war periods. In particular, it is important to explore why the concept of nationhood, especially in relation to Romania, has not been rigorously challenged.

Having lived and worked under two totalitarian regimes – Fascist and Communist – Constantin Noica supported the official ideology of collective identity. He has been seen by many as having a key role in defining national identity in twentieth-century Romanian culture.

In the 1930s, Noica supported Corneliu Codreanu's political ideology, seeing it as the best method of preserving the old Romanian identity:

> The legionaries did not want to create a new Romania. Whoever does not realise this will never understand why Moţa[17] died or the fact that the Captain [of the Iron Guard, Corneliu Codreanu] triumphed so that the Romanian kin may triumph. Foreign rulers could have changed Romania into a different country. Two hundred Swiss technocrats could have told us how to become a different country and told us how to run our business. But can you not see that we are not just talking about new roads and hospitals here? Can you not see that the Romanian spirit is at stake? It is the same Romania that they wanted to revive, even if revival necessitates death.[18]

Noica turned away from reality as he admired the charismatic legionary leader's mystical ideas regarding Romania during this Fascist period. The young philosopher thought these more important than the law, culture and political administration. He retained these beliefs during the Communist era. The spiritual aspects of Romanian identity and language were borrowed from German Romanticism, the confused notions of ethnicity, kin and community transferred from one time period to another.

The same ideas can be found in the essays of Nicolae Iorga, the most renowned of all Romanian historians. Although he had fallen out of favour during the Fascist era due to his allegiance to the royal family, his writings inspired the new generation of intellectuals that emerged during the 1930s and 1940s. In his article in the first ever edition of the newspaper *Neamul românesc* (*Romanian Kin*), Iorga explained that this new publication was needed in order to bridge the gap between private and public interests, between the 'I' and the 'we', so that a collective consciousness could emerge which would determine every initiative, activity or creative act. In the following passage, we can see parallels to Noica's ideas:

> I am writing this not because I am a bearded man, or because I live on a particular street, in a particular house, or because of my particular social position, or because my name begins

with the letter 'I'. It is because I think I am fit to do it, because of my education, my hard work and my spiritual inclination; I feel that I can, therefore, talk about what matters most to our kin, about its needs, its deep longings, its old, sacred suffering, about its lofty aspirations, about everything that greatly affects me as I write this, but also what affects you and your neighbour, and also your enemy, because we are all bound together by one ideal – a clean, fulfilling, everlasting life. Why everlasting? Because even as our own lives will wither, the life of our kin will go on, just as it has done through the ages with God's help, and others will follow in our footsteps, living and toiling like true Romanians. I feel that I can talk about these things not as myself, but on behalf of everyone, because I have greater knowledge than some and therefore I am compelled to speak the longing of all your hearts. Do not think of me as a man who follows his own ends, however pure and righteous they might be, but as someone who works for the common good and pursues a cause greater than myself.[19]

This passage not only reflects Iorga's views, but also foreshadows the mystical rhetoric typical of legionary nationalism and communitarianism. Its exclusivist message gained him widespread popularity. Similarly, Noica's theories about identity do not engage with modern political culture. Instead, they are laden with sentiment untempered by rationality, as we can see in this piece from 1940:

These days we live in a state of grace. Horia Sima does not impose taxes: he galvanises souls. The Minister for Education does not propose reforms in schools: he invests them with a new spiritual dimension. The Romanian community lives in a state of grace. For how long? We will see. It is not only about new laws, but a new state of grace... Only Biblical language can express our current state. We are filled with hope because of this 'grace' or ethnic 'spirit'.[20]

It is clear that the writer is positioning his ideology above the law, which he considers inferior to the movement's spiritual purpose. He claims that education is in a 'state of grace' and therefore does not have to be regulated. Noica was not interested in steering society towards the values of a modern, European form of national identity. His influence on cultural life during Ceaușescu's era was due to the surviving discourse about collectivism, which was encouraged under Romanian Communism. This explains the publication of the texts *Rostirea filozofică românească* (*Romanian Philosophical Musings*, 1970), *Eminescu sau gânduri despre omul deplin al culturii românești* (*Eminescu or Reflections on the Ideal Man in Romanian Culture*, 1975), *Sentimentul românesc al ființei* (*The Romanian Sense of Being*, 1978) and *Cuvânt împreună despre rostirea românească* (*On Romanian Self-Expression*, 1987). The idea of the fictive ethnicity became commonplace in intellectual discourse, overshadowing social realities and failing to challenge the political system.

The influence of Communist-Stalinist ideology was fairly short-lived, and the consciousness of the masses was shaped, to a much greater extent, by ethnoculturalism. This explains the way that the ethnocentrism of the 1930s was effortlessly resurrected in the 1980s. Romanian culture clung to this myth before and after the Second World War. It did not re-evaluate its nationalism through the lens of Marxism or democracy and did not gravitate towards a cultural and political pluralism. Was it the totalitarian regime that hindered the emergence of pluralist discourse? Was it the fault of censorship? Was pluralism avoided out of fear of political unrest or concern that it might divide the community? Was it the oppressive political regime that prevented the re-evaluation of this important subject, which might have been the key to social cohesion? To what extent was the intelligentsia prepared to discuss collective identity? These questions reflect the connection between official political discourse and intellectual debate. Noica was visible in public life during the Communist-nationalist regime, as censorship was reserved only for texts or people who challenged totalitarianism. In the 1980s as in the 1930s and 1940s, Noica was devoted to strengthening the ideal of *ethnos* through his Romantic discourse on the subject of the national community. This ensured that he remained a prominent cultural figure, endorsed by the Communist regime. It is true that he had become more articulate and abandoned some of his old speculations. However, the communitarian message still remained:

In a way, to exist means that 'I am not only myself', that I am something other, and this is where philosophy begins... good can only be achieved through the passivity of the 'I' and its dissolution into the body of the community.[21]

This implies a departure from individualism and a celebration of an abstract 'we'. An imaginary return to communitarianism is preferred to democracy:

Why was the 'I' suddenly corrupted in the nineteenth century? ... After the French Revolution and Hegel, the motto remained 'la chose la mieux partagée du monde' [the most widely shared thing in the world], but it became associated primarily with the revolutionary spirit, rather than the spirit of the community. The 'we' became synonymous with the collective, the administration. In fact, the 'we' was always there, in the shadows, waiting for the 'I' to expose its weakness and hollowness... Individualism lacks philosophical foundations (as Burckhardt's contemporaries readily acknowledged). Any defence of it ignores the distinction between society and community, failing to acknowledge the fact that 'we' comes before 'I' within the social contract and since the Napoleonic crisis, continues to search for something greater than the duality of 'individual and society'. It will be wonderful if, through collectivism, we can rediscover the 'I' that is a part of the 'we', in place of the hollow, lonely 'I'.[22]

It is not only the parallels between the political and intellectual language that are striking here, but also their similar messages, regardless of the context in which they were written. Both promote the idea of national collectivism.

Consequently, it seems that Romanian intellectuals did not challenge totalitarianism because they could not envisage a democratic, liberal alternative; because the ideal of *societas civilis* was absent from public life; because the lack of social pedagogy caused divisions not only within the population, but also within intellectual circles, leading to the paralysis of the critical faculties; because even these intellectuals were seduced by the nationalist ideas promoted through the educational system which prevented them from conceiving an alternative, authentic political culture. Speaking from personal experience, Alina Mungiu-Pippidi writes about the influence of nationalist Communism on the 1980s generation:

> In our famous academic magazine *Opinia studenţească* (*The Student Opinion*) we printed extracts and commentaries on the works of Noica, Cioran and Eliade (whose studies on religion and the interwar era were widely published during this period), proud to have outwitted the censors. Only after 1989, after our main Communist censor Petru Ioan (himself a disciple of Noica's) became a member of a nationalist party and started including *Mein Kampf* on the reading lists of the courses he taught at university, did we realise that we were the ones who had been fooled and played a role we did not fully understand.[23]

Why was this theory of identity so persistently invoked? Romanian intellectuals were blind to the differences between the old patriarchal society and the modern nation that emerged during the interwar period. They did not manage or did not want to distinguish between medieval social relationships and the new order established in Europe by the Enlightenment. The masses were not ready and did not have the social and material means by which to adapt to Western values. Noica and his supporters did not want to endanger the 'sacrosanct ethnolinguistic legitimacy' of the state. Similarly, the majority of the population were reluctant to transform the state on the basis of Western values as they were concerned about losing national sovereignty and their ancestral spiritual roots.

The political analyst István Bibó commented that the small communities of Eastern Europe 'struggled to organise themselves into nations'[24]. Indeed, the idea of the fictive identity conceived by the elite was not easily adopted by the public. The fact that, unlike Western Europe, many populations in Central, Eastern and Southeastern Europe had not had their own states before meant that it was harder for them to reach the same level of political and economic cohesion as countries such as the UK or France. In the beginning, these nations were still affected by the fact that their administration only became centralised in the middle of the nineteenth century. Along with cultural and religious groups, the Romanians had been a part of the Ottoman and Hapsburg empires which not only dominated them politically, but also shaped their values in relation to the interests of their own ruling elites. Western European legal and organisational systems differed from those of Central, Eastern and Southeastern Europe whose regions had been controlled by Vienna and Constantinople. The German principalities were also organised differently than their Eastern neighbours as they were based on the culture of the medieval burgs and their particular constitutional systems. However, there were ideological and political parallels between them, which explains the German influence on the idea of the nation in Poland, the Czech Republic, Hungary, Romania, Serbia, Greece, Bulgaria and Albania. The Czech Republic, Poland and Hungary are special cases, due to the fact that apart from the German influence, they also had their own political traditions and connections to Franco-British political culture.

The German influence – which can be seen in the works of Iorga, Brătianu, Blaga and Noica – not only shaped the ethnonation but created complications due to the problematic intersection of two histories and two essentially different contexts. German Prussian monoculturalism can be seen as incompatible with the multiculturalism, plurilingualism and social and religious norms of the Hapsburg and Ottoman empires. These characteristics reflect the precarious cultural education in Central, Eastern and Southeastern European countries, which hindered the establishment of the political and structural aspects of their nation states. The majority of the citizens of these newly formed nations in the nineteenth century had entirely different histories, traditions, laws and economies from those living in Germany and other Western European countries.

The overemphasis on the German and Western ideal as well as the rushed attempts at modernisation did not benefit the countries of this region. Instead, they resulted in the emergence of ethnocentrist ideologies that fuelled civil wars for over a century. The fascination of the Central, Eastern and Southeastern European intelligentsia with German culture – the Prussian *Volksgeist* – led to the emergence of this fictive ethnicity, and later the German *Süd-Ost Politik*. The UK, France and the US also applied the German ethnonational model when deciding the new Eastern state borders through the Treaty of Versailles.

Although the political situation after the Second World War was similar to that of the interwar period, the old cultural theories of identity were still resonant both for the few academics that challenged Communism and for those devoted to the regimes of Gheorghiu-Dej and Ceaușescu. As far as the masses were concerned, they followed the lead of the new elite, as they had always done, without voicing a different perspective on the notion of collective identity. Nationalism became the meeting point for Communists and former legionaries, Proletkult supporters, and followers of Dej and Ceaușescu, protochronists and followers of the radical Left.

Guided by their own interests, the Communist Party and its leaders encouraged group identity through propaganda and by promoting ethnolinguistic differentialism and monoculturalism. This explains the survival of the ideas of kin and people, which, as we covered in a previous chapter, became inextricably connected to the concept of nation. This ideology was put into action. The Communist regime promoted ethnic exclusivism, as seen through its policies that resulted in the forced exodus of German and Jewish minorities. It came down to selling the people from those groups for a fixed sum and then confiscating their worldly goods. This process was unheard of in recent history and reveals the parallels between the values of Romanian Communists and those on the Far Right. This is the reason why, as Vladimir Tismăneanu argues, Romanian public discourse must be cleansed of its Fascist and collectivist dimensions.

3. THE RETURN TO HERDER

The notion of identity propagated by Noica and his supporters was rooted in Herder's idea of the organic, ethnic nation. Noica continued to promote Herder's historical myth. It is unclear whether he was doing this consciously, but he unmistakably continued to present the institutions of the state and nation as connected. This parallel between Herder and Noica helps us to decode the fantasy of Romanian identity. Noica's allusions to Hegel and his uncritical adoption of Herder's speculations from *Ideen zur Philosophie der Geschichte der Menschheit* reflect the neo-Romantic sources of his beliefs concerning the ethnonation.[25]

The myth of the ancestral spirit of *Volk*, a product of German Romanticism, had a profound and often harmful influence on the intellectual circles of Central, Eastern and Southeastern Europe, even though they were not fully prepared for its impact. Herder's ideas were assimilated indiscriminately and generated the theory of the ethnonation whose ideal form implied a single culture and language, as well as a unique history and geographical space.

The intelligentsia of each region adopted this theory and applied it to their own country, using the same cultural arguments and slogans relating to origins or the historical evolution of collective identity. This fantasy regarding identity and collective rights had the following effects: territorial disputes; spread of cultural and political minorities in various areas of this region; labelling of people living alongside each other in a particular country according to their names, mother tongue and religion, thus nullifying the concept of citizenship; social inequalities; and competing ideological perspectives, all of which claimed to be founded on science.

Herder was one of the first thinkers to discuss Central, Eastern and Southeastern Europe, commenting on the exoticism of the region and outlining its first maps, bringing to the world's attention its particular languages, traditions and folklore. His discoveries seemed so original, even mesmerising to his Western readers – who were in a different phase of civilisation – that they were not concerned with the specifics which Herder could not fully understand. His exaggeration of the uniqueness of Eastern culture and his heavy emphasis on its connection to nature and primitive life became a point of reference for subsequent identity theories. During Herder's time, academics were not equipped to notice the similarities between the religious, administrative and behavioural aspects of various populations from the Balkans. Herder and his Northern or Western European peers did not comprehend the psychology of those communities or the cultural values that formed the basis of life within that region. Enlightenment and Romantic thinkers were unaware that the Orthodox religion possessed the greatest spiritual significance there, much more so than linguistic specificities. Dominating the entire Balkan region, the power of this faith challenged Herder's theory that language is the soul of the people.

Eastern European ethnographic artefacts fascinated Western intellectuals due to their aesthetic qualities and their connections to the ancestral culture, and hence were imagined to possess a deeper connection to the identity of each group than was the case. As for traditions of cuisine or dress, they were even less likely to point to significant ethnonational differences. The specific traditions of the Muslim and Jewish minorities were widely accepted by these pluralistic societies at the end of the eighteenth century. Similarly to other populations that were once part of the Hapsburg Empire, communities in the Balkans became aware of their specific identities relatively late. Even after they achieved independence, they did not immediately seek to assert their distinct social culture. Their ethnicism was borrowed from Herder and other sources, and their later emphasis on ethnographic differences was an artifice used to transform their medieval societies using Western models. In this way, Romanian, Serbian, Bulgarian, Greek and Hungarian intellectuals invoked the ideologies of ethnodifferentialism or ethnocentrism to shape national identity. Many Romanian thinkers have remained faithful to this Romantic culture and its ideological and political ramifications. Nae Ionescu and Noica declared that they belonged to a privileged social group and dismissed the idea of social equality, just like their medieval or boyar ancestors. They insisted that they would save the nation through culture, language and collective identity, thereby justifying their lack of support for social emancipation.[26] This could explain the lack of a civil rights movement in the region. By studying the history of various Romanian cities, it is possible to understand the psychology of the ruling classes and the intellectual elites who supported them.

That Brașov, Timișoara and Sibiu were the sites of the first uprisings against the Communist regime was not only due to the fact that they were more in tune with their diverse cultural heritage, but also because these cities had a *societas civilis* modelled on that of the West. Transylvania and Banat modernised at a faster rate than the extra-Carpathian regions and had preserved this *societas civilis* that enabled them to avoid being entirely overwhelmed by the totalitarian regime and to hold on to some democratic values.[27]

The revolutionary uprising in Timișoara in 1989 surprised leaders of the totalitarian Communist regime and segments of the Romanian intelligentsia because they failed to understand that political change can be motivated by factors besides ethnocultural and national values – and that such protests need not be organised only by known leaders or dissidents, but can be instigated by regular people and social groups believing in a civic culture.

4. THE UNIQUENESS OF ETHNIC CULTURE OR A FURTHER DISCUSSION OF THE IDEA OF NATION

In Romania, the intelligentsia did not encourage the development of the middle classes or steer society in the direction of democracy. Instead, they stressed the importance of the aesthetic dimension without considering the way that spiritual life might be harnessed to benefit society. The ideals of the French Revolution were not embraced by Romanian revolutionaries or the generations that followed. Instead, what developed was a culture antagonistic to diversity. This is amply illustrated by texts written during the second half of the nineteenth century and in the twentieth century. As a result, development of the individual – which was key to achieving the aims of 1848 – was not prioritised.

The division between culture and society was not only typical of Noica's work, but was also supported by many other writers and scientists over the past two centuries. There is nothing unusual about this perspective; there were some exceptions, but this was the general trend. How else are we to explain the limited inclusion in the school curriculum of seminal texts about European democracies? How else are we to interpret the relentless promotion of medieval values that sought to distance the individual from urban norms? How else can we explain the promotion of national values, at the expense of local diversity? These cultural activists belonged to many generations. Nicolae Iorga, Nae Ionescu, Nichifor Crainic and Constantin Noica are just a few of the influential writers who supported ideals of the ruling parties.

In this regard, during the Communist-nationalist regime schools promoted similar ideas to those of the interwar period. They taught collectivist propaganda and rural values, supporting Ceaușescu's 'folkloric myth' whose repercussions can still be felt today as certain segments of society refuse to adopt urban behaviours. This phenomenon has not yet been examined in detail by Romanian philosophers or cultural historians. However, the quest for the revival of a pure form of spirituality through a return to archaic rural ways – and such medieval customs can still be found in certain regions – was the subject of many cultural enterprises. The issue of identity did not seek to 'legitimise the forgetting of the differences' between the old society and new version of the nation, but sought to demonstrate the uniqueness of Volk and its ancient legacy and connect it to the contemporary form of state and nation. It is a mythology, but not a programmatic one;[28] rather a sentimental-Romantic view of the evolution of the nation as well as the nation itself. Such theories, which rely on the continuity of thoughts, traditions, ways of life and means of communication allegedly unchanged by the passage of time, are fundamentally Romantic and tinged with nostalgia for the past.

Seeping into political and cultural life, they impede critical analysis of the history of collectivism, refusing to acknowledge the distinction between the present and the distant or recent past. Political decisions played a part in influencing this cultural message. After changes in cultural paradigms that originated during the eighteenth century, the West consciously emphasised its abandonment of medieval social relations and the old administration controlled by the monarchy, nobility and clergy. It came to terms with the political mutations caused by the English and French revolutions. This break with the past did not occur in Central, Eastern and Southeastern Europe. Consequently, theories of identity in the two halves of Europe differed, just like their historical evolution.

While there is a consensus on these theories, it seems important to discuss once again the ideas of nation and nation state in post-Communist Europe. Minorities threatened by ethnonationalism started to voice their autonomist aspirations after the fall of the Communist dictatorship. The clash between these two forms of identity – those of the majority and of the minorities – indicates a crisis in the nation state. The historian Eric Hobsbawm highlighted this problem: the ethnonational idea of the state as it was conceived in the nineteenth century – relying on ethnic homogeneity – is not only anachronistic, but self-destructive.[29] This is why I believe Romanian nationality should be understood in the legal sense – in relation to citizenship, common territory, social-professional relationships and the rights and obligations determined by political administrations – thereby including German- or Hungarian-speaking minorities, Catholics and Jews within our understanding of Romanian identity regardless of their culture and religious beliefs.

In other words, by approaching the idea of nation through the prism of constitutional patriotism (*Verfassungspatriotismus*) we will avoid ethnic differentialism in politics and state institutions and refrain from placing citizens within a hierarchy on the basis of their number; instead, this kind of nation will embrace multiculturalism and religious differences. By accepting this multiculturalism, we will ensure that every citizen has equal rights. By adopting this position and changing the organisation of our society, we will create a fertile environment for the development of the individual. The idea of the nation will be employed in the service of humanity, and we will accept that the linguistic and religious diversity of its citizens reflects the cultural hybridity shaped by its history.

VI
MULTICULTURAL PHILOSOPHY: A COMPARATIVE PERSPECTIVE

1. THE EDUCATION AND PHILOSOPHY OF MULTICULTURAL DIFFERENTIALISM: OBSERVATIONS ON CHARLES TAYLOR'S PERSPECTIVE

Where does the interest in multiculturalism originate? Was this concept derived from the experience of diverse groups, or were intellectuals misled by speculative politicians? Should the various connotations be analysed from different angles, for instance, by looking at the theories of Western academics and those of Eastern or Southern researchers? While these studies reveal similarities, they also point to the different interpretations of this concept according to region.

Advocates of the teaching and philosophy of multiculturalism claim that all cultures should be integrated and respected, and not marginalised, silenced or oppressed by the dominant culture. According to this theory, individuals or societies are represented by the ideals of particular cultures, grounded in local traditions passed on from one generation to another. They reflect a mentality that derives from the distinct psychological traits of regional, national, linguistic or religious communities. This argument suggests that linguistic differentialism promotes monoculturalism, as it reflects cultural pride, hence creating a connection between national identity and language.

The problem in democratic society is whether cultures that see themselves as ethnically or racially superior should also be respected in this way, especially as they are likely to find themselves in conflict with other cultures. There is a paradox created between the desire to respect these cultures, like all others, and the democratic belief that all individuals should be treated as equals. As a result, we must conclude that there are limits regarding the extent to which every culture can be endorsed.[1]

Charles Taylor analyses the way that political ideas focused on differences develop organically and separately from other ideas that promote universal dignity. The quest for recognition became important when it began to be closely associated with identity. Inspired by the classics of modern philosophy, Taylor argues that recognition is not merely a form of politeness towards other people, but a vital human need. Lack of adequate recognition or misrecognition can act as a form of oppression, marginalisation or exclusion. Taylor points out that dominant groups may enhance their hegemony by portraying minorities or groups with less political or economic power as inferior. Europeans behaved in this way towards different communities during the era of great geographical exploration and again later during the first wave of industrialisation. The experiences of Indians, Filipinos, Africans, Native Americans and others illustrate the way in which the instrumentalisation of oppression has created a strong sense of self-depreciation.

The modern preoccupation with the concept of identity and recognition, Taylor writes, has been the major social change that broke down social hierarchies. In medieval societies, the aristocracy inherited honour due to their position in the social hierarchy. Honour, therefore, was intrinsically linked to inequality. Modern society replaced the idea of honour with that of dignity, an egalitarian and universalist concept. Rousseau was one of the first to criticise the concept of honour based on social hierarchy.

Taylor explains how Rousseau was the first to explore the origins and causes of inequality, stating that corruption and injustice emerge when people begin to seek recognition, distinctions and preferential treatment. This explains how the aspiration for equal rights characteristic of the human being, the Citizen, became a revolutionary aim in 1789 and in all historical moments when the modernisation process required programmes of emancipation. The concept of dignity became not only compatible, but also essential to democratic society.[2]

Taylor connects the development of modern identity with the establishment of a form of politics concerned with differences. He observes that there is a universal theme of differentialism; that everyone is searching for a particular form of recognition, with assimilation being the cardinal sin in the quest for an ideal concept of authenticity. He believes that there are two sides to differentialism – one benign, one malignant. Invoking the originality of the concept of Volk leads to a very complicated area. Taylor writes that the idea of recognition forms the basis of collective identity and, therefore, separatism.[3] Equally plausible is that the subjugation of people and communities generates a need to assert distinctive identities, as can be seen in regions that were previously conquered and colonised, such as America. These motivations are not characteristic of European history. German ethnocultural differentialism does not appeal to the idea of liberation, as Prussia's hegemonic aspirations during the nineteenth century illustrate that it represents the other side of the coin: emergence of the modern ideology of the conqueror whose rights are connected to specific racial characteristics. While its initial goal was the nation state, it became the justification for aggression and desire to conquer. In this way, the concept of Volk steered culture and political thought.

The cultivation by a privileged group of the idea of belonging to a single culture within a conglomeration of communities generated the theory of what Karl Popper called 'neotribalism'. History teaches us that the transition from the medieval to the modern era was characterised by economic development through commerce and industry as well as the emergence of the middle class as the social stratum that embodied the structural transformation of feudal administrations. At the same time, certain aristocratic families and academics endeavoured to sustain theories founded on the superiority of origins, linguistic purity, historical continuity and rights of the first settlers. This explains why most intellectuals and conservative aristocrats have rejected calls for equality and responded by creating theories furthering the cause of inequity. Consequently, there is only a partial connection between the formation of the modern nation or ethnonation and the oppressed ethnic groups' desire for recognition. Jürgen Habermas makes a similar observation, although he does not relate it to the aforementioned German example. According to Charles Taylor, the destructive force of ethnicism (in its worst form, racist, ignorant and radical persecution of minorities) conceived by German culture in the nineteenth century should not be taken into consideration. Without decoding this concept and its connections to the idea of multiculturalism we will fail to understand the values and principles of the politics of recognition. The role played by the concept of ethnicity in nationalist essentialism was not only relevant to the emergence of the first German Reich, but also to Central and Southeastern European nation states. A generalisation based on the example of North America would be inadequate despite the relevance of many of Taylor's points. He asserts that the evolution of identity theory reveals a nationalism that has positive and negative qualities. We see this message, albeit expressed slightly differently, in the work of the historian and political commentator Michel Winock, who coined the terms 'open nationalism' and 'closed nationalism'. His observations raise interesting questions, since the fact that we identify with one group or another does not necessarily imply nationalism, just as differentialism does not always imply respect for others. The controversy relating to multiculturalism is important for this reason, in the same way that analysis of the terms 'ethnic' and 'national' seems to me once again fundamental to the exact circumscription of the same theory.[4]

Aside from these cultural and political evolutions of recognition that are not considered by Taylor, his hypotheses are grounded in careful methodology and solid arguments. First of all, he highlights the idea that broadening and changing the curriculum is essential not so much in the name of a free culture, open to anyone, but rather in the sense of recognising cultures that have been excluded previously. The goal here is the recognition of lost identity: 'The battle for liberty and equality needs to revise its image. The multicultural curriculum means the revision of these images.'[5] As such, there is a connection with challenging presumptions to convey equal respect for all cultures. This 'presumption' implies that the goal of every society is community integration, as every culture has something important to say about the human condition. There is an implied criticism of the traditional curriculum for failing to communicate this:

> But when I call this claim a 'presumption', I mean that it is a starting hypothesis with which we ought to approach the study of any other culture. The validity of the claim has to be demonstrated concretely in the actual study of culture... 'The fusion of horizons' operates through our developing new vocabularies of comparison, by which we can articulate these contrasts.[6]

This invites us to reflect on the partial transformation of our standards, something we owe to our exposure to every culture, as we can discover this 'presumption' in all of them. Aware of the temptation that we might impose our values in interpreting other cultures, Taylor alerts us to the danger of seeing similarities everywhere. This tendency creates false perspectives and hinders recognition. How can we accept the presumption that everyone has their definitive place in the universe? Is this a moral problem? His conclusion is that people do not need to understand their own limits because they and their cultures are only a fragment of human history: 'But what the presumption requires of us is not peremptory and inauthentic judgments of equal value, but a willingness to be open to comparative cultural study of the kind that must displace our horizons in the resulting fusions.'[7]

The image of displaced horizons echoes Gadamer's *Wahrheit und Methode* (*Truth and Method*), and we see similar ideas in holistic philosophy and the Buddhist religion. It seems one of the most generous hypotheses in the field, creating the possibility of escape from the labyrinth of contradictory or confusing interpretations. Multiculturalism is presented not as a divisive force, but as a way of bringing people closer together as they begin to understand one another and work towards a common existential ideal.

2. IDEOLOGICAL MEANINGS OF MULTICULTURALISM: OBSERVATIONS ON HABERMAS'S OBJECTION TO TAYLOR

Not all criticisms of Taylor take into account the fusion of horizons. Some commentators cannot accept multiculturalism and are sceptical of his theories. Jürgen Habermas, for example, finds them too simplistic. Habermas advocates three main dimensions to the discussion of multiculturalism, none of which he thinks is adequately reflected in Taylor's ideology. These dimensions include the philosophical discourse relating to this phenomenon, political correctness and the rights of persecuted minorities. Habermas's dismissal of Taylor's research is perhaps surprising given its extensive engagement with a variety of contemporary concepts. In his view, Taylor does not sufficiently seize upon the role recognition plays in constitutional democracies, focusing mainly on the challenges of intercultural communication within a political and legal context. In my opinion, this criticism seems unjustified and reflects Habermas's personal ideology.

Habermas sees multiculturalism as a sign of social fragmentation, a confused babel of languages aspiring towards globalism, which explains his scepticism concerning its universal cognitive and normative goals. As such, Habermas maintains that every debate about 'the politics of recognition' must be guided by rationality. He adds that an identity based on constitutional principles can be achieved only through preserving the identity of the political community, rather than leading by the nation's cultural orientation. Immigrants should accept the political culture of their new state without trying to impose cultural forms from their mother countries.[8] Habermas does not deny that 'the absence of cultural recognition is correlated with significant social discrimination as the two fuel each other'.[9] He is concerned with the order in which these processes of recognition take place, whether the social act precedes the cultural, or vice versa. In his view, there could be conflict between the two. However, it is important to acknowledge that at times they can be complementary. On the other hand, some analysts insist that if one of these processes of recognition is under way, the other must be subdued or eliminated. Such arguments ignore historical and political realities. Personally, I favour a more open, careful examination.

Habermas agrees with Taylor's view that personal rights are more important than those of a collective. However, he does not agree that liberalism guarantees citizens' ability to choose and act according to their fundamental rights. When conflicts arise, the courts decide who is on the side of truth and the kind of rights they can claim. According to Taylor, each person can benefit from equal rights only if their autonomy is protected, if they can realise the project of their own life. This definition of rights, Habermas observes, is paternalistic as it ignores half of what it means to be autonomous:

> A correct understanding of rights is based on a politics of recognition that protects the integrity of the individual in the context of the life they have built for themselves. This does not require an alternative model that can moderate the system of rights through alternative, normative perspectives.[10]

On the other hand, Habermas believes that the ethnocultural struggle of oppressed minorities opens up a new discussion, as it relates to a different question. He claims that the various liberation movements in multicultural societies do not represent a uniform phenomenon. They point to other problems, the most significant being divisions based on ethnicity, religion and race. These become fundamentalist once there is a regression in the politics of recognition, when they are incensed by a feeling of powerlessness and when there is mass mobilisation that awakens their consciousness and compels them to articulate a new identity.[11] Habermas points out that the nationalism of these minority groups varies by context, and he mentions one case clearly connected to linguistic and ethnic homogeneity. The purpose of this type of nationalism is for the community to preserve its identity, but also to demonstrate that it is a nation capable of political action.

Habermas's historical analogies are not entirely persuasive. In his view, these nationalist movements were modelled on the notion of the state created by the French Revolution. Historical analysis does not fully support this theory. For instance, the French Revolution occurred in a distinct context that did not resemble the majority of European countries and regions, and by ignoring this, we risk drawing flawed conclusions. The uprising occurred in a country with an established statal tradition, where the Enlightenment influenced the social structure and created a middle class. The goals of the Revolution had been to address inequality and, as Taylor has argued, to introduce an egalitarian philosophy established in the late eighteenth century. France had diplomatic traditions and connections with other countries, both in its immediate vicinity and farther afield. Lastly, it had military power and significant influence in Europe. All of these aspects suggest that we must be cautious when drawing parallels between the revolutionary movement in France and social trends in other countries. As Habermas points out, Germany and Italy developed these structures much later, but they also were not fully fledged states. The medieval city states in Germany and Italy were undoubtedly a step towards modernisation, but for a long time their traditions impeded centralisation around a single national identity.

Finally, the German ethnoculturalism that emerged in the eighteenth century (*Aufklärung* has some distinct elements that point to its evolution) and was heavily emphasised during the nineteenth and twentieth centuries did not aspire to the ideal of modernisation promoted by the French Revolution. Moreover, the ethnocultural nation in Germany and Italy preceded the nation state. Habermas concludes his study by pointing out the different influences on the formation of national identity in France and Germany.[12] In the case of Germany, it is the result of a deeply rooted historical process that had a profound influence on ethnic differentialism in all areas possessed by the spirit of *Sturm und Drang*. The cultivation of consciousness contrived by German intellectuals was not seen as necessary in France, even though there was an awareness of the theory of cultural delimitation. In contrast to the concept of *citoyenneté*, *Kulturnation* fostered Germany's intolerance of its neighbours, particularly the French, for over a century. It is widely accepted that these two different principles shaped the identities of their nations.

What are we to make of these philosophical deliberations on the topic of multiculturalism? It was not, as Habermas suggested, French nationalism that created an intelligentsia that craved a specific national and cultural identity, but the ethnonationalism associated with

Volk. French nationalism addressed the consciences of individuals as a philosophy, while the German Romantics and positivists who promoted ethnocultural differentialism had much greater impact on these European states. We only have to turn to the works of the most renowned German philosophers, historians and writers of the nineteenth century to understand the way the German state created that singular, specific version of identity – the ethnonational monoculture. As Habermas illustrates, the exact nature of this specific identity is debatable, but what is certain is that *Volksgeist* fuelled great tragedies of the twentieth century.

During the Romantic and post-Romantic periods, Prussian-German academics preoccupied with the notion of specificity steered the political current towards differentialism. To some extent, a bias towards particularism can be considered acceptable. However, considering the grave inequities it has caused, this theory needs to be scrutinised and reinterpreted. The notion of racial delimitation in a Europe characterised by an intermingled community with a shared history was not only dubious, but it also lacked any scientific basis and should have been rejected by common sense. Heinrich von Treitschke was an intellectual whose enthusiastic support for this notion gained him favour with the German establishment. Other eminent academics exercised their influence over the educational system, which in turn had a lasting impact on society. The history of the interwar era illustrates how the theory of racial specificity could be taken to an extreme and give rise to 'the ideology of death'. For the purpose of our argument, it is important to remember that the process of ethnic purification, in the spirit of serving the majority, destroyed multicultural life in Germany.

Habermas's reservations regarding Taylor's theory of multiculturalism could be due his feeling that it did not go far enough in criticising traditionalism or revising the curriculum. Habermas's references to the emergence of minorities as a result of the formation of nation states in different parts of Europe and the world indicate the importance of a differentiated approach to the phenomenon. This, I admit, is useful in highlighting specific elements of multiculturalism and exploring its complexity. Through his eurocentrism and emphasis on the hegemony of Western culture, Habermas launched an indirect and unfair critical attack on Taylor, who had rejected ideas of domination and cultural subordination and championed the ideal of recognition in every social context.

National and local administration plays its part in resolving conflicts and imposing legal and social norms that allow the peaceful cohabitation of all citizens. Education also has a civic role in encouraging integration. All of these aspects are undoubtedly important, but Habermas's commentary on Taylor's theories completely dismisses the philosophy of multiculturalism or interculturalism. In fact, he argues that neither has a place within liberal society. This is not only an erroneous point of view, but it reflects a dogmatism derived from a conservative perspective on the evolution of cultural values.

He does not investigate the lessons learned from history, nor the consequences of contemporary conflicts. In my opinion, the regions of Europe – probably more than any other part of the world – are characterised by inter-communitarian, multicultural, transcultural and intercultural relationships. Moreover, they are built on traditional cultures that encompass multiple influences and therefore could provide the starting point of a new concept discussed in the following paragraphs – one of multiple identity.

Without discussing specific cases, Habermas focuses his criticism on a single controversial topic in contemporary Germany: the question of asylum seekers. Indeed, this subject is distinct from other discussions of multiculturalism in history. It relates to the emigration of populations from one continent to another in order to escape poverty. Habermas invokes this situation to support his rejection of the early forms of multiculturalism in the United States and Germany in particular. By placing ethnocultural obstacles in the way of immigrants trying to obtain citizenship, the German state sought to protect its old principle of ethnocultural identity. The differentialism inherent in this process played a key role in who was allowed to become naturalised, as it depended on an applicant's ability to prove blood relations with a connection to Germany. It was *jus sanguinis* that gave these people the right to become German citizens. Habermas mentions this briefly and admits that such a view of citizenship dependent on origins is derived from the concept of *Kulturnation*, and that it differs from the definition in other Western European countries, where it is connected to the idea of affiliation.[13] In Germany, the rights of immigrants to become citizens gradually improved, but the concept itself has not been rigorously analysed and the process remains lengthy and bureaucratic. Nevertheless, the connection between the right to citizenship and German ethnicity can be viewed as controversial.

It would have been interesting if Habermas had focused in more detail on the theory of the ethnonation and analysed its manifestation in Germany. For example, he might have compared the monoculturalist and multiculturalist perspectives and the ways in which these shaped modern German society in comparison to Central and Southeastern Europe. If the state of Bismarck still identifies with monoculturalism, it remains to be seen how contemporary intellectuals will forge a mode of communication with the rest of multicultural Europe. I agree with Habermas's view that segregationism is intolerable. But multiculturalism should not be viewed as a step towards segregationism. It is essential that we pay close attention to the case of Germany, given the significant influence that Prussian-German culture has had on Northern, Central and Eastern Europe throughout history. Given the lack of in-depth analysis in Habermas's critique of Taylor, I believe it is crucial to investigate further these problems and conflicts. In conclusion, the identity acquired by some groups has belligerent components, which is why the redefinition of the nation state (especially the ethnonational version based on ethnoculture) needs to take place alongside the discussion of multiculturalism.

Regarded as a consequence of the politics of differences, multiculturalism poses significant challenges in emerging democracies. The first problem is that monocultural and totalitarian traditions are still ingrained in the memories of their people. Second, there are few non-governmental organisations with enough influence to promote cultural and political pluralism. As for the state, its institutions are ill-prepared for such a fundamental reorientation and lack the expertise to garner information about minorities, relevant cultural and legal terminology and multicultural or intercultural education. Both the majority and the minorities are still fascinated by their respective origins, their ties to the land, their archetypes. In other words, they are trapped in a Romantic, premodern era, having failed to engage with the ethos of the Enlightenment. They are not ready for the socio-political or institutional transition that social emancipation requires.

This explains the frequent conflicts between communities within these societies. The former Yugoslavia is not a unique case in Eastern Europe or in other continents. Like Will Kymlicka, Taylor does not focus in detail on specific crises in Central and Southeastern Europe, nor does he have a nuanced understanding of the plight of peoples in the region. A discussion of multiculturalism would benefit from a detailed comparison of Eastern and Western nations, especially as the investigation of this concept has often been confused and marked by partisan interests. Even when we compare the United States and the rest of Europe, we notice similarities as well as differences.

3. HARVEY SIEGEL'S CONTRIBUTION: TRANSCULTURALITY

Openness to the 'other' and their experiences reflects not only the legitimate aspirations of the individual, but also those of the community. By observing interpersonal relationships, it becomes evident that cultures have multiple origins creating a variety of moral values. The transmission of these values from one culture to another depends on the longevity and closeness of their connection and current relationships between different communities. Plurilingualism is a key aspect of this. A systematic analysis of different regions reveals the multiple cultural identities of many societies around the world. In an article on the philosophical ideals of transculturality and their transmission through education, Harvey Siegel makes a terminological distinction that strikes me as particularly convincing. He argues that multiculturalism is legitimate as long as it encompasses both the ideals of a particular culture and those of two or more other cultures simultaneously. He defines this concept as transculturality, which seems a more rational idea than most other theories of multiculturalism.[14]

Siegel explains why multiculturalists embrace a single form of legitimacy that reflects certain philosophical ideals. The result is that these ideals lose their potency outside the closed culture to which they relate.[15] According to Siegel, it would be preferable to assume a multicultural identity that allows us to adapt to different contexts and adopt each new culture as our own, treating its members with due respect. This, he claims, is the only moral way to behave and achieve 'the coherence of the multicultural instinct'.

According to the supporters of multiculturalism, we need to challenge the hegemony of the dominant culture and embark on a process of recognition for each culture to be granted the respect it deserves. The monoculturalist retort is that while the oppression and marginalisation of one culture might seem unjust to its members, it might be considered totally appropriate by the dominant culture.[16] Siegel raises several questions and puts forward various hypotheses on this topic. First, he argues that it is necessary to reformulate multiculturalist demands. Second, he recognises that the rejection of multiculturalism is related to context. Finally, he points out that the ideals of transculturality become more significant once we realise they transcend specific cultures. Siegel describes the transcultural nature of certain normative acts that resulted in recognition and the adoption of this ideal by two or more communities.[17]

Richard Rorty, one of several philosophers who oppose the notion of transcultural ideals, does not think examination of culture requires a common point of reference. In his opinion, the pragmatic course of action would be to privilege one's own group, as ethnocentrism has the potential to build solidarity. Some have inappropriately used his theories to suggest that specificity is the most useful basis for fundamental cultural values. They claim that universalism amounts to nothing more than the protection or imposition of local values. Indeed, it is important to admit there is no such thing as universal values, only local ones. Can the ethnoracialism championed by Rorty and his supporters become a universal concept?

Siegel finds this proposition difficult to accept.[18] First of all, he considers the dichotomy between universal and local as problematic because universalists may choose whether or not to acknowledge particularities within their ideals. Principles, values and ideals are not necessarily tied to local particularities. Siegel also considers this dichotomy to be false because universality cannot be rejected on the basis of local ideals. Additionally, the universal cannot acquire a transhistorical or supersocial dimension, as Richard Rorty and David Theo Goldberg claim.[19] Finally, the legitimacy of transculturality cannot be disregarded by its opponents as long as its overall purpose is the acquisition of knowledge. I tend to agree with Siegel, therefore, that transcultural ideals are tenable. Multiculturalism is entirely compatible with the pursuit of transcendent philosophical and educational ideals. Despite the fact that there are those who argue to the contrary, it seems evident that there are universal ideals embedded in every culture.

4. CONDITIONS LEADING TO FALSE PREMISES OF MULTICULTURALISM

Some misinformation has been disseminated by those who claim the ideals of one group cannot extend to the wider community. We should recall that Romantics such as Herder and Fichte argued that language defines a group's identity.[20] Herder and Fichte's belief that language is an organic component of every human being contributed to the notion of a unique tribe that could be identified through purity of the bloodline. Herder was a vociferous promoter of this vision of culture.[21] Contemporary re-evaluations do not always take into account the Romantics' exclusivist orientation. Is it appropriate to look for parallels between our own socio-political conditions and their historical precedents? Herderianism still appeals to a number of intellectuals who are attracted to his ideas about specificity and who reinterpret them as cultural values. That these Herderian theories are adopted uncritically suggests his legacy is still with us, particularly in regions under Germany's influence and in states where national identity is founded on the concept of ethnicity.

My view is supported by the ideological leanings of many scientific and cultural institutions within post-Communist-nationalist Europe. The impact of this ideology is the preservation of the privileged status of linguistic communities that in the previous century adopted the *Volksgeist* theory and the immense pressure of dividing communities into particular groups, according to whether they belong to the majority or a minority. In the case of Central and Eastern Europe, this has resulted in a mythologisation of the German world despite bilateral political relations that have rarely resulted in 'fair play'. Multiculturalism is critical at this moment in history, but its various facets have still not been fully explored. As cultures cannot be forcibly separated and spiritual life is not tied to a single tradition, it is clear that we must extend the meaning of this term.

In considering the moral dimension of this discourse, we must examine the following questions: do transcultural ideals represent humanity? If the answer is yes, why would we not choose these forms of socio-cultural ideals that reflect the political reality of contemporary life? Why would we choose to interpret multiculturalism as a concept that values specificity and heightens differences within communities? Why not admit that a large number of regions are rooted in a fusion of traditions? The only reason why minorities might oppose this proposition is due to fear of assimilation, while the majority might be concerned about the loss of their authenticity; neither of these appears to me to be credible or morally justifiable.

The supporters of multiculturalism must return to its original premise, namely the legitimacy of every culture and its ability to tolerate the existence of others. In this way, they will realise that others can share their values, as they are transcultural. Even if we cannot always fully detach ourselves from our own culture and integrate within a new one, this should not blind us to the fact that there are values and ideals that transcend specific historical and cultural contexts.

Is it really the case that monolingualism is the only way we can preserve our identity, while plurilingualism necessarily means a break with tradition? Are there really places, regions, states and nations that can only be defined by their connection to a single community, culture, religion or race? Is this the only version of themselves they recognise? A multiculturalism that promotes separatism based on race, ethnoculture, religion and language is irrelevant. The intelligentsia could steer political discussion in a new direction. The supposedly ideal form of expression and way of life the minorities are searching for cannot be achieved without transcultural dialogue. This is the reason why I have reservations about Samuel Huntington's zealous appeal for legislative frameworks regarding the coexistence of multiple identities. The challenges faced by a rapidly changing contemporary society need to be resolved by taking into account the aspirations of minority groups.

5. THE CONCEPT OF MULTIPLE IDENTITY

That in many states around the world – including the most established democracies – we find first- and second-class citizens, persons who are viewed favourably and others who are victims of discrimination, should lead us to be cautious while considering the concept of authenticity. A person's race, their parents' religion, their name or supposed origins can cause them to be excluded and marginalised. By favouring the members of the largest community, freedom of expression has often been restricted and injustice has prevailed, leading to the marginalisation of individuals with a mixed or multiple cultural identity. This phenomenon illustrates the way that ethnoculturalism and multiculturalism can exclude certain minorities, hence it is important to discuss the shortcomings of these two models of thought. The connotations attributed to these terms often reflect a linear, dogmatic perspective of the evolution of an individual or group during their lifetime. This perspective is like a closed circle, and in contemporary society it has led to conflict, alienation and even suicide. It is a point of view that has been adopted by both majority and minority groups.

When academics have offered new, unbiased perspectives on the past and present, they have often found themselves contradicted and ignored by the state and sometimes by civil society, as if they had broached a taboo subject. Often, the state or civil society has redoubled its efforts to promote the prevailing perspective. In the absence of any other points of reference, even the liberal intelligentsia contribute to the perpetuation of these harmful myths. Many official institutions prefer to gloss over unpleasant episodes in the distant or recent past and align themselves with an 'ideology of silence'. This is why I believe that the theory of ethnomulticultural differentialism can be supported by dogmatic thinkers from both sides of the political spectrum. The concept of fixed identity – endorsed by the multiculturalists who believe that the religion we are born into is significant – attempts to draw a continuous line between the two poles that support human existence.

Whether or not this is deliberate, such theories deny the freedom of the individual to move between cultures. The same can occur when individuals have two or more cultural roots, as they often experience uncertainty and discomfort if they feel that a pure cultural identity is seen as superior. As for the ecumenism of the prelates, it seldom materialises in practice, as Pharisaism replaces a more mature, responsible empathic response to other human beings. The disturbing consequences of this include a strained exchange of values, disapproval of mixed marriages and dogmatic intolerance. Undoubtedly, the end result is the incalculable psychological damage experienced by those who are connected with several cultures and languages.

This subgroup of the minority exists and has the same rights to recognition as a majority or a cultural minority. It can serve as a model for cultural groups who see themselves as distinct and superior. Any attempt to impose a narrow notion of identity is so problematic that it would seem wise to discourage rigid categorisation of human beings according to ethnic identity, national identity (both in the context of ethnicity and citizenship) or an identity built on the uniqueness or superiority of a religious doctrine. For as long as we do not admit that these are merely artificial, mutable conventions we will continue to have a superficial, dogmatic perspective on human nature.

The existence of interfaith marriages and multiple identity of their offspring as well as all the customs, traditions and moral values shared by various cultures provide sufficient justification for the development of a concept that addresses the problems mentioned above. By multiple identity, I am referring to a flexible concept that could be used to define the identity of one or more groups. This would create the opportunity for a more coherent 'politics of recognition' that would reject all discriminatory interpretations and practices. Finally, I believe the interfaith and intercultural aspirations of individuals or groups moving frequently between cities, regions, states and continents are damaged by traditionalists within certain religious, cultural and linguistic communities.

The lives and characters of ordinary people reflect the cultural values of contemporary society and are shaped by their changing circumstances. Does the concept of multiple identity present a challenge to the philosophy of politics? A historical approach reveals the indisputable reality of transcultural ideals, particularly in relation to spirituality: they represent a new movement of ideas that attempts to connect the seemingly disparate fundamental landmarks of contemporary thought.

I have discussed how countries bordering states with distinct languages or religions tend to be culturally flexible and open to compromise. In these countries, identity is more relative and there is a greater possibility of accepting the notion of multiple identity. The geography and demography of Europe, Asia and the Americas point to the plausibility of this, as they are characterised by a fusion of traditions resulting from multiple communities living side by side.

Another reason why the concept of multiple identity seems relevant is because the borders between countries were often drawn up arbitrarily, frequently to serve the political interests of a particular group, thus contributing to discrimination. When certain nation states were established after the First World War, some minorities that had been discriminated against became majorities, and took on the role of oppressors. The collapse of empires created ideal conditions for this role reversal as territories were unified or divided, new administrations were put in place and the educational system assumed the role of promoting a uniform identity.

Thereafter, the redistribution of power did not take into account regional, group or personal identities. It lost sight of the significance of the pluralism that had evolved during the course of history. In countries where the intelligentsia were controlled by totalitarian regimes, the abstract ideas of nation and ethnonation gradually replaced regional and civic identities. On the flip side, this concept of ethnicity began to construct a new identity founded on rural rather than urban values. The exception here is Germany, a case that merits closer investigation. The same concept would contribute the marginalisation of any regional particularities that might have enriched the cultures of these modern nations. Similarly to the German example, the unification of states encouraged assimilation and ethnic purity, leading to the marginalisation of minority groups that previously contributed to a pluralist European culture.

Ethnonational ideologies and statal-national administrations built on ethnic criteria have used the discourse of cultural differentialism to bring about irrational programmes concerning the coexistence of multiple identities. Forced assimilation or discrimination were seen as the only alternatives. When it came to certifying the individual in the sense of recognising his membership of a community, the criterion of the bloodline was prioritised above all others. This was used often during the Second World War. Books, magazines, newspapers and, most importantly, the school curriculum contrived to corrode the relationship between different ethnonational groups within nation states. This excessively partisan discourse harnessed every cultural act and used it as political propaganda. According to the wishes of those with political power, a monoculture centred on collective consciousness was constructed, hindering the vital process of modernisation.

Unlike monoculturalism, multiple identity has more positive connotations, similar to those of multiculturalism. How can we define this concept? The common roots of languages and communities suggest that every person has a multiple identity. The areas of social life based on diverse cultural traditions also imply the existence of multiple cultural identity. The most common example is the values that result from the fusion of different elements. Civil society is founded on a pluralist heritage and a mixture of cultures, both premodern and modern. Most importantly, the fusion of spiritual traditions can generate stable common values that form the basis of a 'politics of recognition'. If we choose not to categorise people based on specific criteria such as ethnicity and race, their unique cultural references reveal that they are part of a 'melting pot' where their visions naturally converge. Regional communities are a clear example of this.

Europe's project of unification is aided by its multiple identity. By recognising the identities of people in relation to their region, we adhere to the same political philosophy that promotes the recognition of the rights of religious and linguistic minority groups. What are the most important aspects of regional identity? First, the opportunity of a person of any race, ethnicity or religion to participate in the public sphere. Second, the freedom of any human being to decide what group they wish to belong to. Following on from this premise, it should be possible to identify with more than one such group or tradition, if such a thing were desired. This would create new reference points for regions where several cultures merge. Families with a mixed heritage would aid this process as they would offer a living example of multiculturalism and interculturality.

There is even more to learn by considering regional identity. It conveys an image of human existence based on tacit acceptance of a set of values that act as the backbone of relationships between people, administrative structures and professions. These values are key to peaceful coexistence and can encourage morality as they create a natural connection between the individual's inner consciousness and the outside world. They can also embed themselves in social, professional and institutional spheres.

We began with the idea that the concept of multiple identity can be easily applied to regional life. If we consider the diverse social capital in a specific geographical space, it is possible to understand why a person might have a multiple identity. This can have interesting implications. For example, in the Franco–German world of Alsace, the concomitant use of French, German and Alsatian languages indicates the similarities rather than the differences between people living in this multicultural space. It is possible and indeed essential to coexistence to straddle two different cultures. The establishment of the nation state was historically controversial in Alsace, as it was torn between German occupation and French assimilation. We see the same dynamic at work in Polish–German, Czech–Hungarian, Albanian–Yugoslav, Bulgarian–Turkish and Hungarian–Romanian relations. The idea of compromising natural relations and creating a state of conflict on a regional scale always came from an external power. It took into account the interests of those who claimed the territory, as opposed to inter-community interests.

Attacks on the coexistence of traditions in Tyrol, Adriatic Dalmatia, the southern Czech Republic, Italian-Slovenian Gorizia, Austro-Slovenian Klagenfurt, multilingual Chernivtsi and Romanian-Hungarian Târgu-Mureș suggest that it is time to reinterpret the history and tradition of regional European policy through a different conceptual lens.

The identities of the Belgians, Dutch and Swiss are also part of the same multiple socio-cultural evolution, reflecting a world with fluid frontiers. The communities of the Middle Danube basin and in the Carpathian arc are similar in many ways. It would be misleading to tie the identities of Central-Eastern and Southeastern European regions such as Croatia, Bosnia, Kosovo, Macedonia, Transylvania, Rumelia, Vojvodina and Banat to the concept of ethnicity. Instead of acknowledging these cases, a dominant section of the political leadership imposes the ideology of differentialism and the discriminatory practices it brings.[22] Ideally, we would accept that the coexistence of diverse groups makes ethnonational categorisation impossible. Social, historical and ethnographic studies often have an ideological bias, hence such research does not always give a reliable depiction of reality.

In all the aforementioned regions, the majority group favours assimilation and either treats the minority groups with indifference or offers only a token acknowledgement of their existence and the possibility of a multiple identity. As the educational system has played its part in propagating these uninformed views, there is insufficient awareness that individuals and groups have common interests and share cultural values and social and economic experiences. Most importantly, their coexistence leads to mixed marriages, shared customs and religious cultures, and linguistic assimilations. However, these relationships have always been kept under surveillance and considered suspicious and even disloyal by national or ethnocultural-national administrations keen to preserve the purity of the nation state and the continuity of the ethnonation.

In reality, these administrations placed greater emphasis on family and civic values than the ethnocultural communities whose main concern was their territorial primacy or the nobility of blood. The concept of the township that Alexis de Tocqueville used in relation to American society also played a role in the social coagulation of Europe, as it led to the emancipation of the population and its shift from medieval servitude towards modernisation. In every European civil society or *comunità del popolo* or *bürgerlichegesellschaft* throughout history, the interests, values and aspirations of their people have merged to some extent, suggesting the goal of civic integration is more rational than separatist ideology.

In the same manner as within a town or region, connections can exist between different towns, regions or states. Transculturality can also aid the development of transurban, transregional, transnational and transcontinental relationships. This concept illustrates that the process of integration entails the correlation between education and philosophical ideals. What distinguishes the concept of multiple identity from those of multiculturalism and transculturality is that it rejects the notion of absolute values, challenging any hierarchy based on ethnic, racial, religious or national criteria. If Siegel's transculturality aimed to reveal that 'ideals can transcend individual cultures', then the multiple identity seeks to emphasise the parallels between human values, their common origins and the idea that pluralism might be achieved by inhabiting multiple cultural identities. According to this view, every ideal is relative, hence the conclusion that we should at all times have a comparative perspective of the evolution of the values that shape individual personalities and guide societies. Multiple identity is complementary to multiculturalism, striving to dispel the prejudices that still predominate certain branches of political thought.

We can draw key conclusions based on the analysis and hypotheses in this study and consider the way they can be used to formulate an argument about the aforementioned theories and their practical application: 1) in principle, specificity does not exclude transculturality or multiple identity; 2) this means that a person can embrace the values of their own culture and of other cultures simultaneously; 3) multiculturalism has a logical motivation and a moral basis as long as its purpose is the exchange of values between cultures; 4) transculturality and interculturality lead to the fusion of different world views and can be used to further the aims of multicultural pedagogy; 5) the concepts of transculturality and interculturality are concerned with plurilingual communication as well as personal, civic, regional and multiple identities; 6) not only are diverse cultural roots compatible with coexistence, they can bind together different sections of society; 7) the concepts of transculturality and interculturality can contribute to an accurate interpretation of multiple identity; 8) multiple identity assumes that all cultural, linguistic and religious roots are regarded as equal and that a different identity can be created as these cultural characteristics are transplanted into a new urban, regional or social context; 9) the local/universal dichotomy is no longer relevant once we adopt transcultural, universal values and ideals.[23]

CONCLUSIONS

This book seeks to clarify certain concepts that are relevant not only to the historian or social scientist, but also politicians searching for an alternative ideological position. What is particularly special about this audience? First of all, I feel politicians often portray collective identity in a simplistic and even damaging manner. They have reduced the modern and contemporary community to a series of differences and distinct characteristics, such as tribe, race, kin, ethnicity, nation, religion or language. By merging together certain notions and concepts – for example, identifying ethnicity with tribe or race, or nation with ethnic group and religion – they are responsible for many injustices and false priorities within the historiography and politics of Central and Southeastern Europe. While the concepts of *peuple* and *nation* played a key role in France, the idea of modern collectivity was predominant in Central and Southeastern Europe. This difference in perspective between East and West has had many regrettable consequences, such as social and educational setbacks. Miscommunication between the elite and the masses in the East has consistently stalled the progress of this part of Europe.

Central and Eastern European discourse has employed a range of stereotypes to manipulate the masses, thereby limiting their freedom of thought. This illustrates the contrast between Michelet's and Renan's concept of nation and the direction taken by the German – and later, Greek and Romanian – intelligentsia. The pseudo-religion born out of the intellectual and political currents in Central and Southeastern Europe during the height of nationalism degenerated into an ethnonationalist paranoia in the 1930s and 1940s. In addition to Germany, countries such as Hungary, Bulgaria, Romania, Poland, Serbia and Greece experienced crises of identity during the nineteenth and twentieth centuries as a result of fervent promotion of an ethnocultural differentialism founded on biological racist theories. The conflict that ensued in Yugoslavia as a result of these notions prompted me to investigate their role in the ideology of the whole of Central and Southeastern Europe over the past two centuries. The French model of modern nationality seems particularly valid considering its pale imitations in Eastern Europe. A survey of the notions used to define collective identity in Central and Eastern Europe is rather dispiriting: its discourse has not changed over time, resulting in confusions and conflicts between groups and nations. The simplified, partisan interpretation of the notion of collective identity has contributed to historical turmoil, especially through its propagation of political myths that divide communities and encourage exclusion.

In different contexts, the definition or labelling of collective identities has either slowed down or accelerated the development of individual culture. In the case of the intellectual and political history of Romania, it is directly connected to cultural and political discourse. Cultural analysis reveals that these identity theories are flawed, as they are based on a misreading of the relationship between the majority and minority groups. This meant that the masses were never offered a rational perspective of history. I remember reading nineteenth-century Romanian newspapers in the Academy Library in Bucharest and being struck by the abstruse language and radical ideas formulated by the intellectuals of that era. None of it had any connection to the political arguments of Ernest Renan. I had the same impression while reading Jewish Romanian-language newspapers for my historical research. These two different versions of collective identity – Romanian and Jewish – did not converge because they both suffered from the same shortcomings: their notions of identity ignored reality and the concerns of the other culture.

This book might be viewed as polemical, but my purpose was solely to evaluate and clarify a number of notional problems. My criticisms have been aimed only at those points of view that fail to use an interdisciplinary approach when discussing the phenomenon of identity or do not consult historiographical data when defining nationhood. I wanted to highlight ideological confusion generated by the misapplication of terminology borrowed from other languages and cultures. In particular, I am referring to the way the concept of nation as understood in France and Great Britain has been mechanically transferred to Central and Southeastern Europe, consequently losing its original connotations.

I think the time has come for Central and Eastern European culture to adopt a more nuanced understanding of these concepts, linguistic terms and messages. By analysing the historical, linguistic and ideological roots of the concepts of kin, ethnicity, people and nation, I have tried to suggest a new, more benign definition of collective identity. My studies have led me to conclude that the old Romantic notions regarding collective identity are still very influential, yet education must replace this cultural heritage with alternative concepts that steer us from prejudice.

The current controversies surrounding Romania's past – for example in relation to the Holocaust or the Liberty Statue in Arad – suggest the most important points of our collective history do not only need to be rewritten, but clarified. It is then that multicultural phenomena are revealed, and it is only by coming to terms with them that we can solve current intercultural tensions. This process could lead to a more rational analysis of the political and historical discourse surrounding nationality.

Another conclusion drawn from the theories discussed in this book is that the theme of identity should remain central to political thought. With respect to Central and Southeastern Europe, it is my hope that these regions will use liberal and social democratic principles to redefine collective regional, national and European identity. There is ample justification for abandoning their Far Right and Far Left legacies, and their integration into Europe should motivate them to adopt democratic values, multiculturality and transculturality so that all their citizens can participate equally in social and political life, not to mention the supranational economy.

How might we define Romanian identity? I think it is important to avoid the simplistic merging of terms such as kin and nation or nation and religion. By choosing certain terms we signal our bias towards particular values and dismiss other principles. It seems essential at this moment in time to create a distinction between the state of the citizens and the cultural, linguistic and religious state in Central and Southeastern Europe. This notional clarification is necessary in Romania and will provide a catalyst for a substantial renewal of the national psychology. Only through this will the concept of kin begin to lose its ideological function or sink into oblivion. Finally, I believe that a political system based on a rational, humanist culture will avoid the tragic fate of the former Yugoslavia. The formative role of history and language leads me to conclude that the reform of historiographical and political discourse relies enormously on the prioritisation of conceptual history.

NOTES

Preface

1 Moritz Csáky, *Ideologie der Operette und Wiener Moderne. Ein kulturhistorischer Essay* (*Ideology of the Operetta and Viennese Modernism. A Cultural-Historical Essay*) (Vienna, 1998).

2 Marc Bloch, *Apologie pour l'histoire ou Métier d'historien* (*The Apology of History or the Historian's Craft*) (Paris, 1997).

3 See *Diccionario político y social del siglo XIX español* (*Political and Social Dictionary of 19th-Century Spain*) and *Diccionario político y social del siglo XX español* (*Political and Social Dictionary of 20th-Century Spain*) (Madrid, 2008).

4 Victor Neumann, *Essays on Romanian Intellectual History*, trans. Simona Neumann (2nd edn, Timişoara and Iaşi, 2013).

5 Victor Neumann, *The Temptation of Homo Europaeus: An Intellectual History of Central and Southeastern Europe*, trans. Dana Miu and Neil Titman (edited, revised and updated edn, London, 2020).

Chapter I

1 See Nora 1988.

2 Reinhart Koselleck, 'Volk-Nation', in Brunner, Conze and Koselleck 1992, pp. 141–51; cf. p. 142. Koselleck argues that *das Volk* and *die Nation* are highly abstract concepts that can be applied to a range of different peoples or nations. He sees the concept of democracy as much simpler to define than the ideologies of *das Volk*, *peuple*, people, *popolo*, *popor*, *nép* or *narod*. He suggests the term *das Volk* needs to be deconstructed from a historiographical and philosophical perspective.

3 Nora 1986. This text points to the ideological contradictions and ambivalent use of the aforementioned terms and explains how they must be redefined through historical analysis. See Julliard 1992.

4 Julliard 1992, p. 192. The author argues that *le peuple* was a key concept at the

beginning of the modern era as it referred to four distinct ideas: 1) the birth of a nation opposed to the monarchy; 2) a popular antagonism towards the privileged; 3) the polarisation between workers and those born into wealth; 4) the marginalised poor.

5 Viallaneix 1971, p. 242.

6 Michelet 1974, pp. 227–8.

7 Augustin Thierry, 'Lettres sur l'*Histoire de France*' ('Letters on the *History of France*'), 2e Lettre, pp. 20, 22, in Viallaneix 1971, p. 242.

8 Cf. Viallaneix 1971, p. 244.

9 Jules Michelet, *Histoire de France* (*History of France*), I.I, ch. IV, t. I. p. 70, in Viallaneix 1971, p. 256.

10 Cf. Viallaneix 1971, p. 248.

11 Ibid., p. 250.

12 Ibid.

13 Cf. 'Introduction à l'histoire universelle' ('Introduction to Universal History'), p. 5, in Viallaneix 1971, p. 255.

14 Jules Michelet, *Histoire de la Révolution Française* (*History of the French Revolution*), in Viallaneix 1971, p. 270.

15 Michelet 1974, p. 228.

16 Ibid., p. 230.

17 Ibid., p. 231.

18 Ibid., p. 232.

19 Berlin 2000, p. 116.

20 Ibid., p. 141.

21 For example, he admires the role Providence plays in social relations, particularly with regard to the meaning of life. See Michelet 1853, pp. 19–20.

22 Isaiah Berlin draws attention to the fact that Michelet partially ignores Vico's theory about the cycles of history as well as his anti-democratic inclinations and admiration for primitive, totalitarian societies – in fact, anything that conflicts with his own themes. See Berlin 2000, p. 12. He argues that the mythology formulated by Michelet, in which *le peuple* played a dominant part, was only partially influenced by Vico.

23 Neumann 2001a. See specifically the chapter on Timişoara.

24 See Chapter III.

25 Michelet 1974, p. 160.

26 Ibid., pp. 160–61. For an analysis of the myth of the instinctiveness of the masses, see François Marotin, 'L'instinct du Peuple: Du mythe romantique à l'histoire positive' ('The Instinct of le Peuple: From Romantic Myth to Positive History'), in Bernard-Griffiths and Pessin 1997, pp. 65–76.

27 McKay 1973, p. xx.

28 Ceri Crossley, 'Du sujet libéral au Peuple romantique: conditions de possibilité pour l'éclosion d'un mythe' ('From the Liberal Subject to the Romantic Peuple: Enabling the Birth of a Myth'), in Bernard-Griffiths and Pessin 1997, pp. 117–25 (especially pp. 117–18).

29 Ibid., p. xxvi; see also Nora 1986, p. 38; Julliard 1992, pp. 185–6.

30 Michelet 1974, p. 145.

31 Julliard 1992, p. 204.

32 Neumann 2001a. See the chapter 'Herderianism – Foreshadowing of Ethno-Nationalist Theory?'.

33 Michelet 1974, p. 147.

34 Jules Michelet, 'Cours de 1830–1831, d'après les notes inédites d'un normalien anonyme, Ier leçon' ('Lessons from 1830 to 1831, from the Unpublished Notes of an Anonymous Student of the École Normale, 1st Lesson'), in Viallaneix 1971, p. 260.

35 Viallaneix 1971, p. 265.

36 Reinhart Koselleck proposes the same argument in his study of das Volk and die Nation. Cf. Brunner, Conze and Koselleck 1992, pp. 321–7, in the section 'Exkurs zur Entwicklung der Begriffe "Peuple" und "Nation" in Frankreich 1760–1815' ('Discussion of the Development of the Terms "Peuple" and "Nation" in France 1760–1815'). Unlike other scholars who focus on key concepts from the language of politico-social history, Koselleck notes that the French Revolution introduced Germany to a new style of discourse, but without this resulting in political change. It also did not create the same type of national identity in the two countries. Koselleck adds that the concept of das Volk and die Nation became particularly influential at the beginning of the nineteenth century. The crisis in German identity led to the development of this particular

union of ideas (ibid., p. 327). In short, the French concepts of peuple and nation would take on different semantic connotations in German.

37 Ibid.

Chapter II

1 Berlin 2002, p. 107.

2 These points are made by Sundhaussen 1973, p. 21. The need for a new critical perspective is also proposed in Lemberg 1964.

3 See Neumann 2020, chapters 5 and 6.

4 Johann Gottfried Herder, Anmerkungen [Über den Ursprung der Sprache] (Treatise on the Origin of Language) (1772), in Herder 1973, p. 61.

5 Johann Gottfried Herder, Über die neuere deutsche Literatur. Fragmente (Fragments on Recent German Literature) (1767–8), in ibid., p. 56.

6 Ibid., p. 58.

7 Neumann 1984; cf. Sauder 1984. For a different perspective, see Sundhaussen 1973, pp. 38–40, 41–8.

8 Johann Gottfried Herder, Von Ähnlichkeit der mittlern englischen und deutschen Dichtkunst (On the Resemblance of Medieval English and German Poetry), in Herder 1963, p. 273.

9 Tyrtaeus was a legendary figure from the Second Messenian War, which explains how the poet was perceived in archaic Greek culture. See Compton 2006.

10 Herder 1963, p. 273.

11 Ibid.

12 Palti 1999, especially pp. 322–3. Despite Herder's major contributions to the discovery and representation of Eastern European cultures, we cannot ignore his inconsistent political ideology. Although his theories were widely accepted by the scholars of those countries, they could be seen as an attack on the Ottoman and Hapsburg empires, both of which encouraged cultural diversity. Even today, some theorists discuss the Central, Eastern and Southeastern European concepts of nation through the prism of Volksgeist in its nineteenth-century manifestation.

But to conclude, in the manner of Holm Sundhaussen, that the French variant of national identity did not fit these Eastern regions (with the exception of Hungary) would imply that we accept Herder's evaluation of these empires, despite the fact that he did not suggest an alternative way for their people to live together in harmony. Moreover, it would ignore the role that these political structures played in the social and cultural emancipation of their subjects.

13 Johann Gottfried Herder, *Auch eine Philosophie der Geschichte zur Bildung der Menschheit* (*Another Philosophy of History for the Formation of Humanity*), in Herder 2004, p. 42.

14 Herder 1966, p. 29.

15 Ibid., pp. 90, 95.

16 Ibid., p. 177.

17 Palti 1999.

18 Herder 1966, pp. 350–51.

19 Herder 1935, pp. 38–46.

20 Herder 1966, p. 244.

21 Ibid., pp. 249–50.

22 Johann Gottfried Herder, *Briefe zur Beförderung der Humanität* (*Letters for the Advancement of Humanity*) in Herder 1971, p. 111.

23 Ibid.

24 See Neumann 2020, pp. 163–5.

25 Herder, from *Über die menschliche Unsterblichkeit. Eine Vorlesung* (*On Human Immortality: A Lecture*), in Herder 1973, p. 194.

26 Popper 1996, pp. 27–81.

27 Palti 1999.

28 For a detailed analysis of conceptual history, see the seven volumes of *Geschichtliche Grundbegriffe. Historisches Lexikon zur politisch-sozialen Sprache in Deutschland* (*Fundamental Historical Concepts: Historical Lexicon of Socio-Political Language in Germany*) (1972–97). See Bibliography under Brunner, Conze and Koselleck 1992 (for vol. 7).

29 See Reinhart Koselleck, 'Social History and *Begriffsgeschichte*', in Hampsher-Monk, Tilmans, van Vree 1998, p. 26. Koselleck points out that there is always a difference between the development of history and language in the sense that no spoken act is the act itself. It must be noted that the spoken act contributes to the preparation and fulfilment of the actual act. There are situations in which a word can trigger actions with multiple irrevocable consequences. An obvious example is Hitler's order to invade Poland, where the relationship between the speech and the act itself was clear. Koselleck argues that history is created through society and language, which implies that we would not be able to write a complete history in the style of the Annales School, or more precisely, that of Fernand Braudel. A complete history of society and a complete history of language are mutually exclusive (ibid., p. 25). This overarching concept of history becomes problematic as soon as we admit that the acquisition of knowledge can be a self-correcting process, not an all-encompassing metaphysical system. We feel the same reservations when considering Herder's Romantic attempt to reconstruct universal history. The observation that 'when social history and conceptual history are interrelated, the differences between them undermine each other's claim to universality' (ibid., p. 26) seems to me as one of the great methodological discoveries of the twentieth century, without which it is impossible fully to comprehend historical events, facts and texts. This is another reason why we should not accept wholeheartedly the ideas of those past thinkers who overestimated the role of deterministic theory or constructed a metaphysics of history. According to Koselleck, the anthropological primacy of language in the representation of history indicates that we need it to establish what was and was not linguistically determined in an action from the past (ibid., p. 28).

30 The most important period we can study to analyse the processes that affected society and produced conceptual changes occurred between the sixteenth and nineteenth centuries. It is known as *Sattelzeit*, referring to the historical era during which the transition to modernity began in Western Europe. It encompasses the contributions of the Enlightenment and Romanticism. Perhaps most significant to note is the connection between both movements in relation to Herder's work that was to influence Central and East-Central Europe. The differences between these regions and

the Western states can be easily explained, as their specific historical contexts resulted in varying cultural ideals. However, the overlap between the two aforementioned cultural movements was felt particularly keenly in Central and East-Central Europe, a subject that has not always been addressed. While German conceptual history took into account the arguments made by Koselleck in his 1968 dissertation entitled *Preussen zwischen Reform und Revolution. Allgemeinen Landrecht, Verwaltung und soziale Bewegung von 1791 bis 1848* (*Prussia between Reform and Revolution: General Land Law, Administration and Social Movement from 1791 to 1848*), its English counterpart reflects the impact of the evolution of British political thought as described by J. G. A. Pocock, Gordon J. Schochet and Lois G. Schwoerer in *The Varieties of British Political Thought 1500–1800*. A third example is that of the Dutch – discussed by Pim den Boer in *History of Concepts: Comparative Perspectives* – on the history of the Netherlands in the seventeenth century. Each of these countries has its own distinct history, hence their different interpretation of the same key concepts. In the same book, Iain Hampsher-Monk draws attention to the distinctions between English and German conceptual history ('Speech Acts, Languages or Conceptual History?', in Hampsher-Monk, Tilmans, van Vree 1998, pp. 37–50), while Pim den Boer describes German and British influences on specific features of the Dutch language and culture, concluding that this resulted in an amalgamation of traditions ('The Historiography of German Begriffgeschichte and the Dutch Project of Conceptual History', in ibid., pp. 13–22). What do we learn from studying the conceptual history of *Sattelzeit*? There are four distinct processes that affect societies as they begin their journey towards modernisation: 1. location; 2. democratisation; 3. ideology (leading to concepts replacing concrete social and historical references); 4. politicisation. According to this definition, Herder's texts relate to location, ideology and politicisation.

Chapter III

1 Raoul Girardet, 'Présentation' ('Introduction'), in Renan 1996, p. 223.

2 See ibid., pp. 161–87.

3 Ibid., pp. 224–5.

4 Noiriel 1996, p. 11.

5 In response to this question, modern French historians including François Furet and Pierre Nora have discredited the idea of a clear connection between two historical periods that are so different and separated by such a long time. Nora argued that the idea of the nation did not have the connotations of solidarity, collective consciousness or political structure that it acquired in 1789. See Nora 1988, pp. 803–4.

6 Renan 1996, p. 228.

7 Ibid., pp. 228–9.

8 Hobsbawm 1996, p. 135.

9 Renan 1996, p. 231.

10 Weiss 1997, pp. 64–79, 80–96.

11 Renan 1996, p. 233.

12 Ibid. My italics.

13 Berlin 1997, p. 175.

14 Renan 1996, pp. 234–5.

15 Berlin 1997, pp. 224–5; see also Berlin 2000, pp. 221–42.

16 Renan 1996, p. 236.

17 Ibid., p. 237.

18 See also Noiriel 1996, pp. 39–41.

19 Cf. Dvornichenko 1993. There are striking similarities between the history of Ukraine and that of Moldova, Wallachia and Transylvania.

20 Cf. Koselleck 1996. For a fresh perspective on this topic, see Koselleck 2002. The term *Begriffsgeschichte* (conceptual history) has come to define a new discipline championed by a group of German researchers. In addition to Otto Brunner's work, it is important to acknowledge the contributions of Reinhart Koselleck of Bielefeld University, who collaborated with Brunner and Werner Conze on *Geschichtliche Grundbegriffe. Historisches Lexikon zur politisch-sozialen Sprache in Deutschland* (*Fundamental Historical Concepts: Historical Lexicon of Socio-Political Language in Germany*) (see Chapter II, note 28, and Bibliography under Brunner, Conze and Koselleck 1992 (for vol. 7)).

21 Prizel 1998, p. 14.

22 Ernest Renan, *La Guerre entre la France et l'Allemagne* (*The War between France and Germany*), in Renan 1996, p. 186.

23 This debate on identity continues in German academic and political circles. When the question of German reunification arose, it emerged that there was still a lack of consensus regarding the concept of nation. The prospect of new German unity created an identity crisis. The controversy culminated in the famous *Historikerstreit* ('Historians' dispute') in 1987. The study of German history in schools was seen as a solution to the identity crisis. In a 1986 article in the *Frankfurter Allgemeine Zeitung*, historian Ernst Nolte urged the people of Germany to put to rest the overwhelming guilt of their Nazi past, pointing out that the resulting 'negative nationalism' threatened the very legitimacy of Federal Germany. See Bettina Westle, 'Collective Identification in Western and Eastern Germany', in Kriesi, Armingeon, Siegrist and Wimmer 1999, p. 178.

24 This is particularly important in redefining the concept of nation. See Reinhart Koselleck's commentary in Koselleck 1996, p. 60.

25 Prizel 1998, pp. 19–26. See also Hanspeter Kriesi, 'Introduction: State Formation and Nation Building in the Swiss Case', in Kriesi, Armingeon, Siegrist and Wimmer 1999, pp. 13–31.

26 On the other hand, many intellectuals are still wedded to the concept of national identity, which they see as thriving. See Josep R. Llobera's analysis of national and European identities in Llobera 1993.

27 Cf. Max Haller, 'Voiceless Submission or Deliberate Choice? European Integration and the Relation between National and European Identity', in Kriesi, Armingeon, Siegrist and Wimmer 1999, pp. 263–96. See also the chapter on the philosophy of multiculturalism, which contains a paragraph on the significance of 'multiple identities' and their impact on the social, cultural and linguistic character of several European regions.

28 Tamás 1994.

29 Renan 1996, p. 239. For an analysis of ethnonationalism in Eastern Europe, see Danilo Kiš, 'On Nationalism', in Thompson 1992, p. 332.

30 Janicki 1995.

31 Tismăneanu 1998, p. 154.

32 Prizel 1998, pp. 28–9.

Chapter IV

1 Herzfeld 2001.

2 Koselleck 2000, p. 12.

3 Herzfeld 2001, pp. 40, 53.

4 Paleologu 1997, pp. 20–21.

5 See Niculescu 1993.

6 Linguists, ethnographers and anthropologists do not always display a clear perspective on these matters, as their pluralist bias means that they often resort to pure speculation. At other times they express themselves through metaphors rather than rational arguments. The only way of gaining a true understanding of these matters is through detailed historical study, using the tools conceived in the Enlightenment. Among the *Aufklärer*, Nikolaus Vogt claimed that 'the "heroic mania" of princes should be attenuated... lest historians might be tempted to turn into philosophers'. I am aware of the ambiguity of this concept, the oscillation between progress and downfall; in other words, everything that creates the ideological function of history. According to Koselleck, this type of reasoning surpasses ideology. See Koselleck 1997, p. 97.

7 See Neumann 2020.

8 Wagner 2003.

9 Livezeanu 1998, p. 179.

10 Alexandrescu 1998, pp. 68–9.

11 Noica 1940a; see Florian and Petculescu 1994, pp. 316–17.

12 Gellner 1983.

13 Hitchins 1996, p. 21. To quote it in full: 'They [the Romanian politicians in 1848] defined the state as a nation with a stable identity... *Inspired by the modern idea of the ethnic nation*, they aspired to a vision of a greater Romania that included Romanians from the Habsburg and Tsarist empires... [T]he Transylvanian revolutionaries, like

their brethren on the other side of the Carpathians, believed in the ideal of the ethnic nation.' The political discourse on the topic of ethnicity adopted at the time by some Romanians was not promoting a modern definition of identity akin to the political ideal conceived in Revolutionary France by Michelet. In other words, there was no equivalence between the rhetoric used in Paris and the one used in Blaj, Bucharest and Islaz. There were instances, however, when Romanian revolutionaries proposed ideologies that had the same civic connotations as *populus* or *peuple*. The first, more liberal, phase of the revolution in Wallachia was abandoned in the following decades in favour of a movement that was conservative rather than 'modern', as Hitchins claims. Pompiliu Teodor discusses this question in Teodor 2000. (Teodor influenced Hitchins during his studies in Cluj, and this can be interpreted as the reason for the Transylvanian bias in his analysis of the problem of collective identity.) For an explanation of the German Romantic influence on Eastern European concepts of ethnicity, see Victor Neumann, 'Herderianismul: o prefigurare a teoriei etnonaționaliste?' ('Herderianism: A Precursor to Ethnonationalist Theory?'), in Neumann 2001a, pp. 9–29. For an analysis of the rhetoric of Romanian revolutionaries, see Paul Cornea, 'Cuvântul popor în epoca pașoptistă: sinonimii, polisemii și conotații. Între semantica istorică și semiotica mentalului colectiv' ('The Word *Popor* in the Forty-Eighters Revolution: Synonyms, Polysemy and Connotations: On Historical Semantics and the Semiotics of the Collective Mind'), in Cornea, Paul 1980, p. 230.

14 See Chapter III.

15 Cornea, Andrei 2003, p. 149.

16 Cornea, Paul 1980, p. 230.

17 Cipariu 1848. See Mitu 1997, p. 219.

18 Barițiu 1843. See Mitu 1997, p. 219.

19 Vasile Conta, 'Chestiunea evreească' ('The Jewish Question'), in Conta 1914, pp. 647, 648, 658. Cf. Neumann 2018, pp. 181–4. Nearly a century later, like Conta, Florin Cântec also proposes a confused and poorly argued ethnoracial ideology in Cântec 2002. The following passage illustrates his

response to Conta's ideas: 'Discussing the various ethnic conflicts over the course of history that have involved the Jews, Conta concludes that their integration into society is harmful and dangerous for the young Romanian state. His argument was based on "scientific" knowledge and had a profound impact when it was delivered in a speech to the Romanian Parliament in 1879. To dismiss it as merely racist would be an error.' The sentence is all the more surprising as its author denies the evidence. This is another reason why I believe the intellectual history of ideas deserves a special place in Romanian studies and scientific debates. The meanings behind the fundamental notions that define identity only partly account for the ignorance and serious conceptual confusions that are perpetuated from one generation to another. No matter how well intentioned, and regardless of which cultural, political or state group such sentimental statements champion, they limit objective analysis and the historian's freedom of expression. In my opinion, the study of Romanian history and of the history of the cultural-linguistic and religious minorities reveals one and the same theme: the history of Romania. As for the nation – in the modern sense, a state-administrative form permitting all inhabitants the status of equal and free citizens – it legitimises itself as a subject of study from the moment it is expressed through laws, that is, by a constitution.

20 Popovici 1939, pp. 65–7.

21 Neumann 2002, and Andrei Roth's analysis of Popovici's nationalist ideology in Roth 1999.

22 Niculescu 1997. See also Niculescu 1998.

23 Nicolae Iorga, 'Conștiința națională românească de la Mihai Viteazul pînă astăzi. Două conferințe făcute parlamentarilor ardeleni' ('The Romanian National Consciousness from Michael the Brave to the Present Day: Two Lectures Delivered to Transylvanian Parliamentarians'), in Iorga 1987, pp. 198–9.

24 Ibid., p. 213.

25 Nicolae Iorga, 'Unitatea națională în literatura românească' ('National Unity in Romanian Literature'), lecture given

at the Congress of the Cultural League in Timişoara, in Iorga 1987, pp. 264–5. See Claudio Magris's comments about Iorga's obsession with the idea of origins in Magris 1986, as well as Sorin Mitu's observations on the preoccupation of nineteenth-century Transylvanian scholars with Romania's origins in Mitu 1997, pp. 260–82.

26 Ionescu 1930. See Florian and Petculescu 1994, pp. 195–7. For the development of mystical nationalism and cultural stereotypes in interwar Romania, see especially Volovici 1991.

27 Cuza 1928. See Florian and Petculescu 1994, pp. 192–3.

28 Arhivele Statului Bucureşti. Fond Preşedinţia Consiliului de Miniştri (Bucharest State Archives, Presidency of the Council of Ministers), file 479/1941, f. 66. See Benjamin 1993, pp. xxxix–xl.

29 Arhivele Statului Bucureşti. Fond Preşedinţia Consiliului de Miniştri (Bucharest State Archives, Presidency of the Council of Ministers), file 484/1941, f. 66. See also Benjamin 1995.

30 See Niculescu 1997.

Chapter V

1 Hitchins 1996; Ornea 1999; Livezeanu 1995; Pászka 1999; Tismăneanu 1998; Voicu 2000.

2 See Smith 2004, pp. 99–100.

3 Ionescu 1997, p. 158.

4 Voicu 2000, pp. 60–61.

5 Botta 1937. See Florian and Petculescu 1994, pp. 247–8.

6 Cioran 1937. See Florian and Petculescu 1994, pp. 249–50.

7 Iliescu 2005.

8 See Neumann 2002. See also Neumann 2013, pp. 71–113.

9 Laignel-Lavastine 1998.

10 See Chapter IV, section 3 ('The racial connotations of kin'), where I discuss the racist connotations of the concept of kin in Iorga's philosophy.

11 Crainic 1940. See Florian and Petculescu 1994, pp. 301–4. See also the detailed analysis in Ornea 1999, pp. 87–113.

12 Laignel-Lavastine 1998, pp. 328–58, the chapter 'Beyond Nihilism: Romanian Views on Europe and its Destiny'. Nicolae Ceauşescu's Communist-nationalist regime was anti-European. The regime's suspicion of any connection with the world beyond Romania was illustrated by the fact that it banned books that explored the European origins of the ideas of Romanian thinkers during the eighteenth and nineteenth centuries. This was the case with my book *The Temptation of Homo Europaeus*, which was excluded by the Ministry of Culture from Eminescu Press's list from 1988 to 1989. It has been published since 1989 in many editions, both in Romanian and English: Ştiinţifică Press, Bucharest, 1991; Boulder, Colorado, and Columbia University Press, New York, 1993; All Press, Bucharest, 1997; Scala Arts & Heritage Publishers, London, 2020.

13 Ornea 1999, p. 220.

14 Ionescu 1937a, p. 201.

15 Ionescu 1937b. See Florian and Petculescu 1994, p. 259.

16 Laignel-Lavastine 1998.

17 The Moţa–Marin legionary corps was founded in 1938 by Corneliu Codreanu, playing the role of an elite paramilitary organisation of 10,000 members. Their motto was 'Ready to die'.

18 Noica 1940b. See Florian and Petculescu 1994, pp. 304–5.

19 Iorga 1906.

20 Noica 1940c. See Ornea 1999, p. 218.

21 Noica 1987, p. 13.

22 Noica 1993, pp. 151–2.

23 Mungiu-Pippidi 2003, p. 120.

24 Bibó 1986.

25 See Chapter II.

26 Laignel-Lavastine 1998, p. 45.

27 Victor Neumann, 'Cultura civică a Timişoarei în anii dictaturii naţional-comuniste. O evoluţie pe coordonatele Europei Centrale' ('The Civic Culture of Timişoara during the National-Communist Dictatorship: An Evolution on the Coordinates of Central Europe'), in Neumann 2001a, pp. 149–75.

28 Laignel-Lavastine 1998, p. 172.

29 Hobsbawm 1990, pp. 63–7.

Chapter VI

1 Amy Gutmann, introduction to Taylor, Appiah, Habermas, Rockefeller, Walzer and Wolf 1994, p. 5.

2 Charles Taylor, 'The Politics of Recognition', in Taylor, Appiah, Habermas, Rockefeller, Walzer and Wolf 1994, pp. 26–7.

3 Ibid., p. 30.

4 First, the concept of ethnicity may relate to racial elements that can be found in many cultures. Second, even when defined simply as common psychological traits, this concept can still lead to divisions and violent conflicts. It reveals an impulse to preserve certain values at all costs and reject the psychology of differences. In states where the ethnic majority defines national identity, the presence of ethnic minorities is unsettling and there is rejection of cultural pluralism, which is often seen as imposed on them by the outside world. The third aspect of this question is that current proponents of ethnocentrism use the concept of *das Volk* as a signifier for the original cultural community and give it mythical status, which often offends their neighbours as it translates into eccentric outbursts and irrational political aspirations. The study of sociology, history and the philosophy of history illustrates that no group (*das Volk*) can claim cultural purity (and certainly not racial purity) as it inhabits a restricted space and lives alongside other groups (*die Völker*). Germany, which inspired this ideology and sustained it during the nineteenth and twentieth centuries, is itself a place where different worlds and influences converge and combine to create a spiritually fertile environment. The Jewish and Slavic populations have had a significant influence on German culture. In addition, it is those states whose democracies are most unstable (where civic culture, equality, freedom and human rights are less apparent) that have adopted the notion of identitarianism (*Volksgeist*) from Prussian-German culture, using it to create deceptive narratives of history, the concept of the nation or regional issues in the name of collective rights. This notion of original culture has resulted not only in verbal aggression, but also wars whose consequences can still be felt. By rejecting a socio-political system based on legal and civic identity and promoting ethnic separatism, over the past two centuries some states have created divisions seemingly impossible to repair. We must not forget that in countries that modernised late or too quickly, a minority (not always an elite, as they see themselves) has benefited enormously from distorting reality in this way or creating a state of agitation through the pseudo-theory of purism. In some cases, they compromise all moral values in the name of collective ethnicity. In Eastern Europe, for instance, they are still the cause of its late or incomplete emancipation; see also Chapter III.

5 Taylor, Appiah, Habermas, Rockefeller, Walzer and Wolf 1994, p. 65.

6 Ibid., pp. 66–7.

7 Ibid., p. 73.

8 Jürgen Habermas, 'Struggles for Recognition in the Democratic Constitutional States', in Taylor, Appiah, Habermas, Rockefeller, Walzer and Wolf 1994, pp. 107–48.

9 Ibid., p. 110.

10 Ibid., p. 113.

11 Ibid., p. 145.

12 Ibid.

13 See also ibid., p. 146.

14 Siegel 1999.

15 Ibid., pp. 393–4.

16 Ibid., p. 396.

17 Ibid., p. 402.

18 Ibid., pp. 402–3.

19 Ibid., p. 404: 'Goldberg's (and Rorty's) denial of universality relies upon the presupposition that values, in order to be universal or transcultural, must be grounded in some impossibly neutral perspective. He argues, in effect, as follows: 1. Universal (moral) principles and values must be grounded on, or derived from, a "transhistorical or supersocial Godly" perspective. 2. There is no such perspective. 3. Therefore, there can be no universal principles or values. If universalism is

understood in this way, then I agree with Goldberg and Rorty that there can be no such universal values, principles or ideals. But we need not and should not understand the term in this way.'

20 Neumann 2001b. Cf. Neumann 2001a, pp. 9–30.

21 By viewing Herder's work as the origin of contemporary pluralist theory we ignore that he was the first to promote the concept of *Volksgeist*, which became the main justification of the nationalist conflicts in the nineteenth and early twentieth centuries. This notion can also be challenged by close study of his texts and the substantial research on Herder's speculations. See also the commentary on Herderian pluralism in Linker 2000.

22 See, for example, Diplich 1960 and Neumann 1997. By considering identity from a regional perspective, particularly in relation to border regions, it is possible to create a vision of the nation state that does not rely on ethnography or culture. In his study of the Polish and German minorities in the border region of Flatow-Złotów, Mathias Niendorf came to similar conclusions as I did in my research on Banat. His findings suggest that the rigidly nationalist twentieth-century interpretation of the nation state was flawed. See Niendorf 1997. I believe that contemporary political and cultural philosophy needs to redefine European identity for the future.

23 This section of the study was completed during my research in the United States as a Fulbright Scholar between 2000 and 2001. I am grateful to the late Professor George McLean, my partner at The Catholic University of America, Washington, DC, for giving me the opportunity to work at several prestigious institutions in the United States and inviting me to a ten-week international seminar on the theme of multiculturalism.

BIBLIOGRAPHY

Alexandrescu 1998. Sorin Alexandrescu, *Paradoxul român* (*The Romanian Paradox*) (Bucharest, 1998).

Barițiu 1843. Gheorghe Barițiu, 'Ce este panvalahismul?' ('What is Panvalahism?'), in *Foaie pentru minte, inimă și literatură* (*Writings on the Mind, Heart and Literature*) VI (1843), pp. 42–3.

Benjamin 1993. *Evreii din România între anii 1940–1944* (*The Jews in Romania 1940–1944*), vol. 1, *Legislația antievreiască* (*Anti-Jewish Legislation*), ed. Lya Benjamin (Bucharest, 1993).

Benjamin 1995. Lya Benjamin, 'The Racial Definition of Jewishness in Romanian Legislation (1938–1944)', in *Anuarul Institutului de Istorie Cluj-Napoca* (*Periodical of the Institute of History Cluj-Napoca*), vol. 34 (1995), p. 133.

Berlin 1997. Isaiah Berlin, *The Crooked Timber of Humanity: Chapters in the History of Ideas*, ed. Henry Hardy (Princeton, 1997).

Berlin 2000. Isaiah Berlin, *Three Critics of the Enlightenment: Vico, Hamann, Herder*, ed. Henry Hardy (Princeton and Oxford, 2000).

Berlin 2002. Isaiah Berlin, *Four Essays on Liberty* (Oxford, 2002).

Bernard-Griffiths and Pessin 1997. *Peuple, Mythe et Histoire*, ed. Simone Bernard-Griffiths and Alain Pessin (Toulouse, 1997).

Bibó 1986. István Bibó, *A kelet Európai kisállamok nyomorúsága* (*The Miseries of Small Eastern European States*), in Bibó, *Összegyűjtött Munkái* (*The Complete Works*), vol. 1 (Munich, 1986), pp. 202–52.

Botta 1937. Dan Botta, 'Țara analfabetă' ('The Illiterate Country'), in *Buna vestire* (*Good Tidings*), year I, no. 7 (28 February 1937).

Brunner, Conze and Koselleck 1992. *Geschichtliche Grundbegriffe. Historisches Lexikon zur politisch-sozialen Sprache in Deutschland* (*Fundamental Historical Concepts: Historical Lexicon of Socio-Political Language in Germany*), vol. 7, ed. Otto Brunner, Werner Conze and Reinhart Koselleck (Stuttgart, 1992).

Cântec 2002. Florin Cântec, 'Vasile Conta and the Jewish Question' I–II, *Cronica* (*Chronicle*), 11 (2002), pp. 12–13, and 12 (2002), p. 12.

Cioran 1937. Emil Cioran, 'Renunțarea la libertate' ('Renouncing Liberty'), in *Vremea* (*The Weather*), X, no. 480 (21 March 1937).

Cipariu 1848. Timotei Cipariu, 'Uniunea' ('The Union'), in *Organul luminării* (*The Tool of Enlightenment*), II, no. 67 (1848), p. 381.

Compton 2006. Todd M. Compton, *Victim of the Muses: Poet as Scapegoat, Warrior and Hero in Greco-Roman and Indo-European Myth and History* (Washington, DC, 2006).

Conta 1914. Vasile Conta, *Opere complete* (*Complete Works*) (Bucharest, 1914).

Cornea, Andrei 2003. Andrei Cornea, *Turnirul khazar. Împotriva relativismului contemporan* (*The Khazar Tournament: Against Contemporary Relativism*) (2nd edn, Iași, 2003).

Cornea, Paul 1980. Paul Cornea, *Regula jocului* (*The Rule of the Game*) (Bucharest, 1980).

Crainic 1940. Nichifor Crainic, 'O nouă misiune' ('A New Mission'), in *Revista Fundațiilor Regale* (*Royal Foundations Review*), VI, no. 9 (1 September 1940).

Cuza 1928. Alexandru C. Cuza, 'Doctrina naționalistă creștină. Cuzismul' ('Christian Nationalist Ideology: Cuzism'), in *Apărarea națională* (*National Defence*), VI (15 and 16 April 1928).

Diplich 1960. Hans Diplich, *Rumänisch-Deutsche Kulturbeziehungen im Banat und Rumänische Volkslieder* (Romanian-German Cultural Relations in Banat and Popular Romanian Songs) (Freiburg, 1960).

Dvornichenko 1993. Andrei Dvornichenko, 'Istoriia Ukrainy I problema srednovekovoi vostochno-slavianskoi Gosudarstvennosti' ('The History of Ukraine and the Medieval Problem of East Slavic Statehood'), in *Vestnik Sankt-Peterburgskogo Universiteta* (*Saint Petersburg University Bulletin*), Series 2: *Istoria, Iazykoznanie, Literaturovedenie* (History, Linguistics, Literary Criticism) (1993), no. 3, pp. 13–24.

Florian and Petculescu 1994. Alexandru Florian and Constantin Petculescu, *Ideea care ucide. Dimensiunile ideologiei legionare* (*The Fatal Idea: The Dimensions of Legionary Ideology*) (Bucharest, 1994).

Gellner 1983. Ernest Gellner, *Nations and Nationalism: New Perspectives on the Past* (Oxford, 1983).

Hampsher-Monk, Tilmans, van Vree 1998. *History of Concepts: Comparative Perspectives,* ed. Iain Hampsher-Monk, Karin Tilmans, Frank van Vree (Amsterdam, 1998).

Herder 1935. Johann Gottfried Herder, *Geist der Völker* (Jena, 1935).

Herder 1963. Johann Gottfried Herder, *Herders Werke*, vol. 2 (Weimar, 1963).

Herder 1966. Johann Gottfried Herder, *Outlines of a Philosophy of the History of Man*, trans. T. Churchill (New York, 1966).

Herder 1971. Johann Gottfried Herder, *Herders Werke in fünf Bänden (Works of Herder in Five Volumes)*, vol. 1 (Berlin a nd Weimar, 1971).

Herder 1973. Johann Gottfried Herder, *Scrieri despre limbă și poezie, filozofia istoriei, ideea de umanitate, geniu și educație, precedate de un jurnal (Essays on Language and Poetry, the Philosophy of History, the Concept of Humanity, Genius and Education, Prefaced by a Journal)*, trans. and introduction by Cristina Petrescu (Bucharest, 1973).

Herder 2004. Johann Gottfried Herder, *Another Philosophy of History and Selected Political Writings*, trans., introduction and notes by Ioannis D. Evrigenis and Daniel Pellerin (Indianapolis and Cambridge, 2004).

Herzfeld 2001. Michael Herzfeld, 'Vers une phénoménologie ethnographique de l'esprit grec' ('Towards an Ethnographic Phenomenology of the Greek Spirit'), in *Les Usages politiques du passé (Political Uses of the Past)*, ed. François Hartog and Jacques Revel (Paris, 2001), pp. 39–53.

Hitchins 1996. Keith Hitchins, *România 1866–1947*, trans. George G. Potra and Delia Răzdolescu (Bucharest, 1996). Original English edition: *Rumania 1866–1947* (Oxford, 1994).

Hobsbawm 1990. Eric Hobsbawm, *Nations and Nationalism since 1780: Programme, Myth, Reality* (Cambridge, 1990).

Hobsbawm 1996. Eric Hobsbawm, *The Age of Revolution: 1789–1848* (New York, 1996).

Iliescu 2005. Adrian-Paul Iliescu, 'Elitismul ca refuz al diversității' ('Elitism as an Opposition to Diversity'), in *Cultura (Culture)*, no. 8 (49) (2–8 March 2005), p. 10.

Ionescu 1930. Nae Ionescu, 'De la Sămănătorul la noul stat românesc' ('From the Sower to the New Romanian State'), in *Cuvântul (The Word)*, year VI, no. 1907 (13 August 1930).

Ionescu 1937a. Nae Ionescu, *Roza vînturilor (The Rose of the Wind)* (Bucharest, 1937).

Ionescu 1937b. Nae Ionescu, 'Naționalism și Ortodoxie' ('Nationalism and Orthodoxy') in *Predania (Tradition)*, I, nos. 8–9 (1–15 June 1937).

Ionescu 1997. Nae Ionescu, *Introducere în istoria logicei (An Introduction to the History of Logic)* (Bucharest, 1997).

Iorga 1906. Nicolae Iorga, 'Către cetitori' ('To the Readers'), in *Neamul românesc (Romanian Kin)*, no. 1 (10 May 1906), pp. 1–3.

Iorga 1987. Nicolae Iorga, *Conferințe. Ideea unității românești (Lectures: The Idea of Romanian Unity)*, ed. Ștefan Lemny and Rodica Rotaru, afterword, notes and bibliography by Ștefan Lemny (Bucharest, 1987).

Janicki 1995. Lech Janicki, 'Status Mniejszosci Narodowych w Konstytucjach Krajow Srodkowo-I Wschodnioeuropejskich' ('The Status of Ethnic Minorites and the Constitutions of Central and Eastern European Countries') in *Przegląd Zachodni (West Review)*, no. 51 (1995), pp. 43–55.

Julliard 1992. Jacques Julliard, 'Le Peuple' ('The People'), in *Les Lieux de mémoire (Realms of Memory)*, vol. 3 (Paris, 1992), pp. 185–229.

Koselleck 1996. Reinhart Koselleck, *The Meaning of Historical Terms and Concepts: New Studies on Begriffsgeschichte*, ed. Hartmut Lehmann and Martin Richter, German Historical Institute Washington, DC, Occasional Paper no. 15 (1996), pp. 50–60.

Koselleck 1997. Reinhart Koselleck, *L'Expérience de l'Histoire (The Experience of History)*, trans. Alexandre Escudier, Diane Meur, Marie-Claire Hoock and Jochen Hoock (Paris, 1997).

Koselleck 2000. Reinhart Koselleck, *Zeitschichten: Studien zur Historik (Layers of Time: Studies in History)* (Frankfurt am Main, 2000).

Koselleck 2002. Reinhart Koselleck, *The Practice of Conceptual History: Timing History, Spacing History*, trans. Todd Samuel Pressner, foreword by Hayden White (Stanford, 2002).

Kriesi, Armingeon, Siegrist and Wimmer 1999. Hanspeter Kriesi, Klaus Armingeon, Hannes Siegrist, Andreas Wimmer (eds),

Nation and National Identity: The European
Experience in Perspective (Zürich, 1999).

Laignel-Lavastine 1998. Alexandra
Laignel-Lavastine, Filozofie și Naționalism:
Paradoxul Noica (Philosophy and Nationalism:
The Noica Paradox), trans. Emanoil Marcu
(Bucharest, 1998).

Lemberg 1964. Eugen Lemberg,
Nationalismus (Nationalism), vol. 1, Psychologie
und Geschichte (Psychology and History),
and vol. 2, Soziologie und politische Pedagogik
(Sociology and Political Teaching)
(Hamburg, 1964).

Linker 2000. Damon Linker, 'The Reluctant
Pluralism of J. G. Herder', in The Review of
Politics, 62.2 (Spring 2000), pp. 267–93.

Livezeanu 1995. Irina Livezeanu, Cultural
Politics in Greater Romania: Regionalism,
Nation Building, and Ethnic Struggle, 1918–1930
(Ithaca, NY, 1995).

Livezeanu 1998. Irina Livezeanu, Cultură și
naționalism în România Mare 1918–1930 (Culture
and Nationalism in Greater Romania 1918–1930)
(Bucharest, 1998).

Llobera 1993. Josep R. Llobera, 'The Role
of the State and the Nation in Europe', in
European Identity and the Search for Legitimacy,
ed. Soledad Garcia (London and New York,
1993), pp. 64–81.

Magris 1986. Claudio Magris, Danubio
(Danube) (Milan, 1986).

McKay 1973. John P. McKay, The People by
Jules Michelet, trans. and introduction by
John P. McKay (Chicago and London, 1973).

Michelet 1853. Jules Michelet, Principes de
la Philosophie de l'histoire, traduits de la Scienza
Nuova et précédés d'un discours sur le système et
la vie de l'auteur par Jules Michelet (Principles of
the Philosophy of History, Translated from the
Scienza Nuova and Preceded by a Study of the
Author's System and Life by Jules Michelet)
(Brussels, 1853).

Michelet 1974. Jules Michelet, Le Peuple
(The People), introduction and notes by
Paul Viallaneix (Paris, 1974).

Mitu 1997. Sorin Mitu, Geneza identității
naționale la românii ardeleni (The Genesis
of National Identity of the Romanians of
Transylvania) (Bucharest, 1997).

Mungiu-Pippidi 2003. Alina Mungiu-
Pippidi, 'Între clădirea respectului de sine

și respectul sinelui. Dificila redresare a
intelectualului român după Ceaușescu'
('Creating Self-Respect, Creating the
Self: The Difficult Period of Transition of
Romanian Intellectuals after the Fall of
Ceaușescu'), in Intelectualul român față cu
inacțiunea (The Romanian Intellectual and the
Absence of Action), ed. Mircea Vasilescu,
afterword by Adrian Cioroianu (Bucharest,
2003), pp. 111–21.

Neumann 1984. Victor Neumann,
Convergențe spirituale (Spiritual Convergences)
(Bucharest, 1984).

Neumann 1997. Victor Neumann, Identités
multiples dans l'Europe des régions. L'Interculturalité
du Banat (Multiple Identities in the Europe
of Regions: The Interculturality of Banat)
(Timișoara, 1997).

Neumann 2001a. Victor Neumann, Ideologie
și Fantasmagorie (Ideology and Phantasmagoria)
(Iași, 2001).

Neumann 2001b. Victor Neumann, 'National
Political Cultures and Regime Changes
in East-Central Europe', in The History of
Political Thought in National Context, ed. Iain
Hampsher-Monk and Dario Castiglione
(Cambridge, 2001), pp. 228–46.

Neumann 2002. Victor Neumann,
'Federalism and Nationalism in the Austro-
Hungarian Monarchy: Aurel C. Popovici's
Theory', in East European Politics and Societies,
vol. 16, no. 3 (2002), pp. 864–98.

Neumann 2013. Victor Neumann, Essays
on Romanian Intellectual History, trans. Simona
Neumann (2nd edn, Timișoara
and Iași, 2013).

Neumann 2018. Victor Neumann, Istoria
evreilor din România. Studii documentare și
teoretice (The History of Jews in Romania:
Documentary and Theoretical Studies)
(Bucharest, 2018).

Neumann 2020. Victor Neumann, The
Temptation of Homo Europaeus: An Intellectual
History of Central and Southeastern Europe,
trans. Dana Miu and Neil Titman (edited,
revised and updated edn, London, 2020).

Niculescu 1993. Alexandru Niculescu,
'Nația și limba' ('Nation and Language'),
in România Literară (Literary Romania),
no. 42 (1993), p. 3.

Niculescu 1997. Alexandru Niculescu,
'Neamul: Considerații filologice și nu numai'

('Kin: Philological Theories and Other Concepts'), in *România literară* (*Literary Romania*), no. 45 (1997), p. 3.

Niculescu 1998. Alexandru Niculescu, 'Naționalitate și Naționalism' ('Nationality and Nationalism'), in *Euphorion*, no. 1 (1998), p. 6.

Niendorf 1997. Mathias Niendorf, *Minderheiten an der Grenze: Deutsche und Polen in den Kreisen Flatow (Złotów) und Zempelburg (Sępólno Krajeńskie) 1900–1939* (*Minorities at the Border: Germans and Poles in the Flatow (Złotów) and Zempelburg (Sępólno Krajeńskie) Districts 1900–1939*) (Wiesbaden, 1997).

Noica 1940a. Constantin Noica, 'Întâlnirea de la 6 octombrie' ('The Meeting of 6 October') in *Buna Vestire* (*Good Tidings*), year IV, no. 25 (6 October 1940).

Noica 1940b. Constantin Noica, 'Fiți înfricoșător de buni' ('Be Frighteningly Good'), in *Buna Vestire* (*Good Tidings*), year IV, no. 2 (10 September 1940).

Noica 1940c. Constantin Noica, 'Sunteți sub har' ('A State of Grace'), in *Buna Vestire* (*Good Tidings*), year IV, no. 20 (4 October 1940).

Noica 1987. Constantin Noica, *Cuvânt împreună despre rostirea românească* (*On Romanian Self-Expression*) (Bucharest, 1987).

Noica 1993. Constantin Noica, *Modelul cultural european* (*The European Cultural Model*) (Bucharest, 1993).

Noiriel 1996. Gérard Noiriel, *The French Melting Pot: Immigration, Citizenship, and National Identity*, trans. Geoffroy de Laforcade, foreword by Charles Tilly (Minneapolis, 1996).

Nora 1986. Pierre Nora, *Présentation, Les Lieux de mémoire* (*Introduction, The Realms of Memory*), vol. 2 (Paris, 1986), pp. 35–8.

Nora 1988. Pierre Nora, 'Nation', in François Furet and Mona Ozouf, *Dictionnaire critique de la Révolution Française* (*Critical Dictionary of the French Revolution*) (Paris, 1988), pp. 801–11.

Ornea 1999. Zigu Ornea, *The Romanian Extreme Right: The Nineteen Thirties*, trans. Eugenia Maria Popescu (New York, 1999).

Paleologu 1997. Alexandru Paleologu, 'Balcanicul Socrate și socraticul Caragiale' ('The Balkan Socrates and the Socratic Caragiale'), in *Secolul 20* (*20th Century*),

nos. 7–9 (*Balcanismul*) (*Balkanism*) (1997), pp. 20–21.

Palti 1999. Elias Palti, 'The "Metaphor of Life"': Herder's Philosophy of History and Uneven Developments in Late Eighteenth-Century Natural Sciences', in *History and Theory: Studies in the Philosophy of History* (Wesleyan University), vol. 38, no. 3 (1999), pp. 322–47.

Pászka 1999. Imre Pászka, *A román hivatáselit. Identitás- és legitimitásválság* (*The Romanian Professional Elite: The Transition of Identity and Legitimacy*) (Budapest, 1999).

Popovici 1906. Aurel C. Popovici, *Die Vereinigten Staaten von Groß-Österreich. Politische Studien zur Lösung der nationalen Fragen und Staatsrechtlichen Krisen in Österreich-Ungarn* (*The United States of Greater Austria: Political Studies on the Solution to National Questions and Constitutional Crises in Austria-Hungary*) (Leipzig, 1906).

Popovici 1939. Aurel C. Popovici, *Stat și Națiune: Statele Unite ale Austriei Mari* (*State and Nation: The United States of Greater Austria*), trans. Petre Pandrea (Bucharest, 1939).

Popper 1996. Karl Popper, *The Open Society and Its Enemies*, vol. 2, *The High Tide of Prophecy: Hegel, Marx and the Aftermath* (London, 1996).

Prizel 1998. Ilya Prizel, *National Identity and Foreign Policy: Nationalism and Leadership in Poland, Russia and Ukraine* (Cambridge, 1998).

Renan 1996. Ernest Renan, *Qu'est-ce qu'une Nation? et autres écrits politiques* (*What is a Nation? and Other Political Writings*) (Paris, 1996).

Roth 1999. Andrei Roth, *Naționalism sau Democrație* (*Nationalism or Democracy*) (Târgu-Mureș, 1999).

Sauder 1984. Gerhard Sauder, 'Die deutsche Literatur des Sturm und Drang. Zum Begriff Sturm und Drang' ('The German Literature of *Sturm und Drang*: On the Term *Sturm und Drang*'), in *Europäische Aufklärung* (*European Enlightenment*), vol. II, ed. Heinz-Joachim Müllenbrock (Wiesbaden, 1984), pp. 327–78.

Siegel 1999. Harvey Siegel, 'Multiculturalism and the Possibility of Transcultural Educational and Philosophical Ideals', in *Philosophy, the Journal of The Royal Institute of Philosophy*, vol. 74, no. 289 (1999), pp. 387–409.

Smith 2004. Anthony Smith, *Nationalism: Theory, Ideology, History* (Cambridge, 2004).

Sundhaussen 1973. Holm Sundhaussen, *Der Einfluss der Herderschen Ideen auf die Nationsbildung bei den Völkern der Habsburger Monarchie (The Influence of Herder's Ideas on Nation Building among the Peoples of the Hapsburg Monarchy)* (Munich, 1973).

Tamás 1994. Gáspár M. Tamás, 'Old Enemies and New: A Philosophic Postscript to Nationalism', in *Studies in East European Thought*, no. 46 (1994).

Taylor, Appiah, Habermas, Rockefeller, Walzer and Wolf 1994. Charles Taylor, K. Anthony Appiah, Jürgen Habermas, Stephen C. Rockefeller, Michael Walzer and Susan Wolf, *Multiculturalism: Examining the Politics of Recognition*, ed. Amy Gutmann (Princeton, 1994).

Teodor 2000. Pompiliu Teodor, *Samuil Micu. Istoricul (Samuil Micu: The Historian)* (Cluj, 2000).

Thompson 1992. Mark Thompson, *A Paper House: The Ending of Yugoslavia*, ed. Mark Thompson (New York, 1992).

Tismăneanu 1998. Vladimir Tismăneanu, *Fantasies of Salvation: Democracy, Nationalism, and Myth in Post-Communist Europe* (Princeton, 1998).

Viallaneix 1971. Paul Viallaneix, *La Voie royale. Essai sur l'idée de Peuple dans l'œuvre de Michelet (The Royal Way: Essay on the Concept of the People in the Work of Michelet)* (new edition, Paris, 1971).

Voicu 2000. George Voicu, *Mitul Nae Ionescu (The Myth of Nae Ionescu)* (Bucharest, 2000).

Volovici 1991. Leon Volovici, *Nationalist Ideology and Antisemitism: The Case of Romanian Intellectuals in the 1930s* (Oxford and New York, 1991).

Wagner 2003. Richard Wagner, 'Europa de Est, stat federal american?' ('Eastern Europe, American Federal State?'), trans. Carmen Nicolaescu, in *Observator Cultural (Cultural Observer)*, no. 182 (19 August 2003), p. 19.

Weiss 1997. John Weiss, *Ideology of Death: Why the Holocaust Happened in Germany* (Chicago, 1997).

INDEX

Neam, popor sau naţiune? Despre identităţi politice europene was originally published by Curtea Veche, Bucharest, in 2003. This new translation is based on the text of the third edition, published by Editura RAO, Bucharest, in 2015, with the addition of a new preface by the author.

© Victor Neumann 2003, 2015
Preface © Victor Neumann 2021

This edition © 2021 by
Scala Arts & Heritage Publishers Ltd
27 Old Gloucester Street
London WC1N 3AX, United Kingdom
www.scalapublishers.com

ISBN 978-1-78551-374-9

Translated by Gabi Reigh
Edited by Neil Titman

Dust jacket and binding design
by Dieter Penteliuc-Cotoşman
Interior book design by Linda Lundin
Printed and bound in Turkey

10 9 8 7 6 5 4 3 2 1

All rights reserved. No part of this book may be reproduced, stored in a retrieval system or transmitted in any form or by any means, electronic, mechanical, photocopying, recording or otherwise, without the written permission of the author and publisher.